1

CAT. 64
INCOMPLETE OPEN CUBES, 1974/1982
122 PAINTED WOODEN STRUCTURES AND
PENCIL ON PAINTED WOODEN BASE
STRCUTURES: 2 5/8 X 2 5/8 X 2 5/8" EACH
BASE: 29 X 70 X 65"
THE LEWITT COLLECTION,
COURTESY OF THE WADSWORTH ATHENEUM
MUSEUM OF ART, HARTFORD

PREVIOUS PAGE: CAT. 64 - DETAIL

2

SOL LEWITT:
INCOMPLETE OPEN CUBES

EDITED BY NICHOLAS BAUME

WITH ESSAYS BY NICHOLAS BAUME, JONATHAN FLATLEY, AND PAMELA M. LEE

THE WADSWORTH ATHENEUM MUSEUM OF ART HARTFORD, CONNECTICUT

THE MIT PRESS CAMBRIDGE, MASSACHUSETTS LONDON, ENGLAND

PUBLISHED BY THE WADSWORTH ATHENEUM MUSEUM OF ART
IN CONJUNCTION WITH THE EXHIBITION:
SOL LEWITT: INCOMPLETE OPEN CUBES

ORGANIZED BY THE WADSWORTH ATHENEUM MUSEUM OF ART
EXHIBITION CURATOR, NICHOLAS BAUME

WADSWORTH ATHENEUM MUSEUM OF ART,
HARTFORD, CONNECTICUT: JANUARY 26 - APRIL 29, 2001
COLBY COLLEGE MUSEUM OF ART,
WATERVILLE, MAINE: JULY 8 - AUGUST 26, 2001
THE CLEVELAND MUSEUM OF ART,
CLEVELAND, OHIO: SEPTEMBER 23 - DECEMBER 30, 2001
SCOTTSDALE MUSEUM OF CONTEMPORARY ART,
SCOTTSDALE, ARIZONA: JANUARY 18 - APRIL 14, 2002

DESIGNED BY vBUREAU.COM

PRINTED BY MERIDIAN PRINTING, RHODE ISLAND

PHOTOGRAPHY CREDITS:
SEAN MCENTEE, PP. 23 (MUYBRIDGE), 31
JOHN GROO, PP. 1, 2, 6, 16, 17, 33-41, 46, 63-73, 80, 112
DICK LOESCH, PP. 74-5
IAN REEVES, PP. 104-5
THE ANDY WARHOL FOUNDATION INC./ ART RESOURCE, NY, PP. 89-90
TOM VAN EYNDE, PP. 42-43

LIBRARY OF CONGRESS
CATALOGING-IN-PUBLICATION DATA

SOL LEWITT:
INCOMPLETE OPEN CUBES / EDITED BY NICHOLAS BAUME;
WITH ESSAYS BY NICHOLAS BAUME,
JONATHAN FLATLEY,
AND PAMELA M. LEE.
P. CM.
INCLUDES BIBLIOGRAPHICAL REFERENCES.
ISBN 0-262-52311-6 (PBK. : ALK. PAPER)
1. LEWITT, SOL, 1928- .INCOMPLETE OPEN CUBES.
2. LEWITT, SOL, 1928—CRITICISM AND INTERPRETATION.
3. CONCEPTUAL ART—UNITED STATES.
4. CUBE IN ART.
5. WHITE IN ART.
I. LEWITT SOL, 1928-
II. BAUME, NICHOLAS.
III. FLATLEY, JONATHAN.
IV. LEE, PAMELA M.

N6537.L46 A68 2001
709'.2—DC21   00-051125

CONTENTS

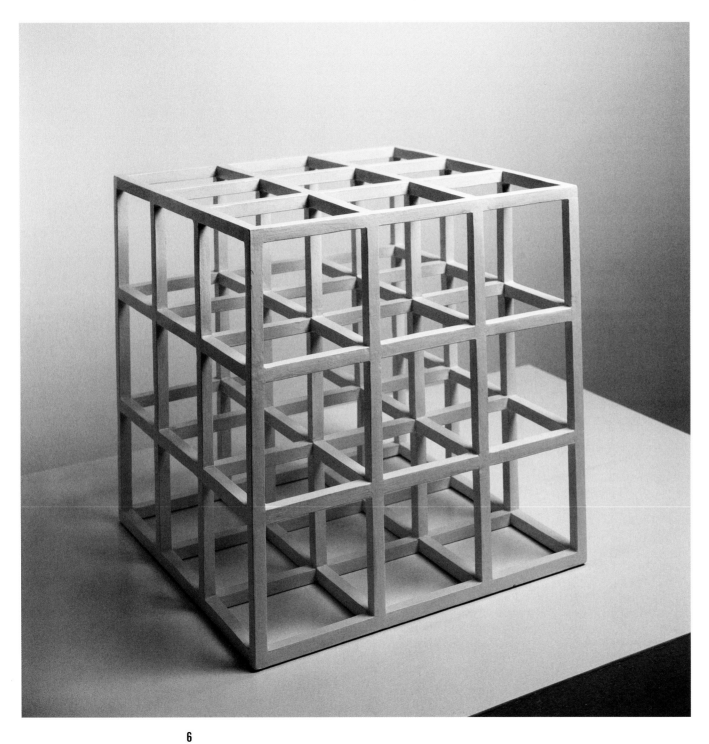

CAT. 1
MODULAR CUBE, 1965
PAINTED WOOD
14 1/2 X 14 1/2 X 14 1/2"
THE LEWITT COLLECTION,
COURTESY OF THE WADSWORTH ATHENEUM
MUSEUM OF ART, HARTFORD

FOREWORD

Sol LeWitt is one of the most influential artists of his generation. His four-decade career has been celebrated through an extraordinary number of major exhibitions, including the recent retrospective organized by the San Francisco Museum of Modern Art. The potency of LeWitt's life's work has in no way diminished with age. His long and close association with the Wadsworth Atheneum Museum of Art has inspired this exhibition and publication, *Sol LeWitt: Incomplete Open Cubes*, which explores in detail one of the artist's most important bodies of work.

Born in Hartford in 1928, Sol Le Witt began his close ties to the Wadsworth Atheneum when he attended art classes here as a young boy. Today, audiences can see a wide range of works by LeWitt at the Atheneum, including four permanent installations of wall drawings spanning the artist's career. LeWitt's broad influence on contemporary art is due not only to his powerful body of work, but also to his close friendship with and support of other artists. Over the years, Sol and his wife Carol Androccio LeWitt, have built their art collection, trading with and buying the work of his fellow artists. The Wadsworth Atheneum has been honored to display segments of this preeminent collection, which includes LeWitt's American and European contemporaries as well as emerging artists. Portions of the collection have been on long term loan to the Wadsworth Atheneum since the 1970s, and have inspired many exhibitions over the years.

A pioneer of minimal and conceptual art in the 1960s and 1970s, LeWitt created work that has come to represent avant-garde art of that period. His sculptures — or structures as he prefers to call them — defined the movement that turned away from representational painting to an abstract art that represented objectivity. LeWitt's *Variations of Incomplete Open Cubes*, made in 1974, represents both a turning point in his art and an embodiment of many of the central artistic concerns of the era.

The exhibition was conceived and organized by Nicholas Baume, Emily Hall Tremaine Curator of Contemporary Art at the Wadsworth Atheneum. It brings together thirty large-scale variations lent by museums and private collections around the world. These sculptures have been installed throughout the museum's galleries, allowing for comparisons among different works in the series as well as with the art and architecture of earlier centuries. A small-scale version of the entire series is also featured along with the artist's freehand and schematic drawings, many of these exhibited for the first time. Following its Hartford showing, the exhibition will travel to Colby College Museum of Art, Maine; The Cleveland Museum of Art, Ohio; and the Scottsdale Museum of Contemporary Art, Arizona. We are indebted to the lenders for their generosity in sharing their works with the public and thereby ensuring the exhibition's success.

We wish to thank the exhibition sponsors for their generous assistance. *Sol LeWitt: Incomplete Open Cubes* is made possible by The Helen M. Saunders Charitable Foundation, Agnes and William R. Peelle, Jr., and The Ritter Foundation. Additional support has been provided by The Pryor Foundation, Nancy and Robinson Grover, and The Richard Florsheim Art Fund.

Kate M. Sellers
Director, Wadsworth Atheneum Museum of Art

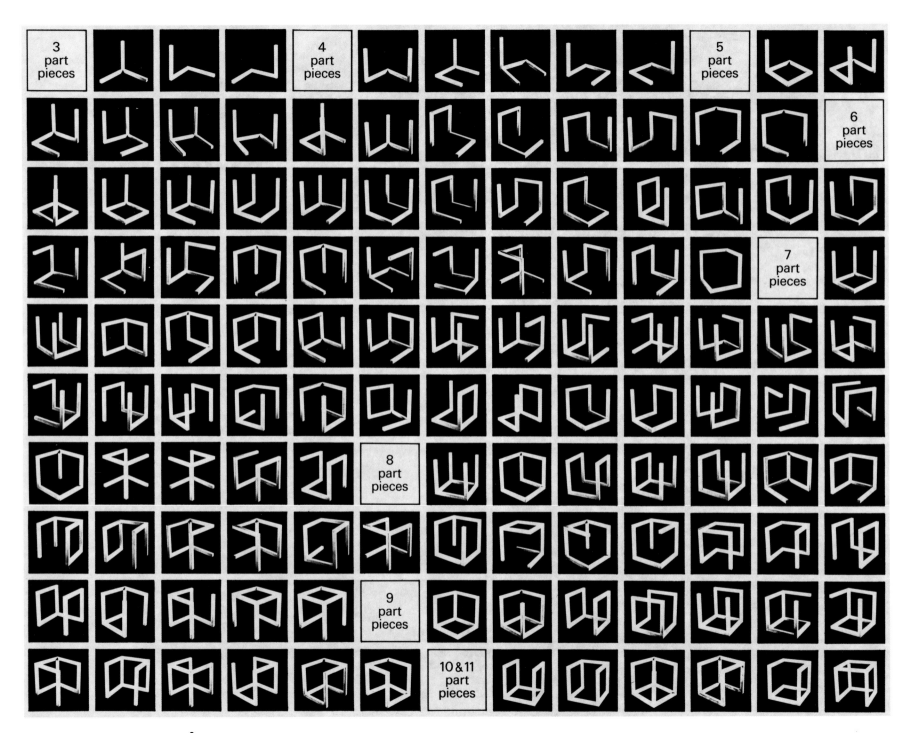

ACKNOWLEDGMENTS

The considerable appeal of major retrospectives, all-encompassing surveys and broad thematic exhibitions notwithstanding, it is a rare pleasure to focus an exhibition and publication on a single work of art. It is particularly rewarding when the work in question is as densely formulated, richly expressed and historically significant as Sol LeWitt's *Variations of Incomplete Open Cubes*.

I was introduced to LeWitt's work by John Kaldor, the Australian collector and patron whose family, as luck would have it, lived next-door to my own when I was growing up. I remember being both fascinated and perplexed as I observed a large, oddly shaped white geometric structure that had appeared in the library of the Kaldor home, a late-nineteenth century gothic-revival villa on the shores of Sydney Harbor. It turned out to be *Incomplete Open Cube 7/21*, one of 122 variations on the theme of an incomplete open cube. The hold on my imagination of this strangely incongruous object only grew as I continued to look; the encounter generated that kind of pivotal aesthetic experience that finds in an object the surprising and powerful condensation of sense and form.

Although the series is most succinctly referred to as *Incomplete Open Cubes*, the full title begins, *"Variations of..."* These variations are explored in detail in the essays that follow and, in other ways, in the exhibition's installation at the Wadsworth Atheneum and at subsequent venues. With the works distributed throughout the permanent collection galleries, the notion of variation relates not only to the relational differences among LeWitt's structures, but also to their comparative differences from the art and architecture of earlier periods.

This unconventional approach to the installation presented many challenges. I am indebted to Betsy Kornhauser who, as Chief Curator and later Acting Director, was an enthusiastic advocate for the exhibition. Judy Kim, Assistant Curator of Contemporary Art, contributed with customary intelligence and precision to many aspects of the exhibition's development. Janet Passehl, Curator and Registrar of The LeWitt Collection, facilitated my research and supervised the preparation of many works for inclusion in the exhibition with characteristic professionalism, insight and unfailing good humor. Susanna Singer, LeWitt's long-time associate, provided essential information on the location of works and typically wise counsel on a range of topics.

I am delighted that this book presents fresh responses to LeWitt's art from a younger generation of writers, as well as documenting many works for the first time. In my essay, "The Music of Forgetting," I introduce *Incomplete Open Cubes* and offer a detailed descriptive analysis of its conception, execution and critical reception. In their contributions, Pamela M. Lee and Jonathan Flatley widen the discussion of LeWitt's work through comparative analyses. Lee's "Phase Piece" explores the structure of *Variations of Incomplete Open Cubes* in relation to the musical notion of phasing, a technique associated with the "minimalist" composer Steve Reich. Flatley's "Art Machine" explores LeWitt's and Andy Warhol's shared aspiration to identify an alternative to subjective choice as the ordering principle for artistic expression. Flatley finds *Incomplete Open Cubes* to be the paradigmatic example of a deployment of seriality more about pleasure and emotion than cognition.

My great thanks to editorial consultant Marcia Hinckley, who read each of the essays with characteristic perceptiveness and offered many constructive suggestions. I am further indebted to Douglas Crimp, Jonathan Flatley, James Meyer and Andrea

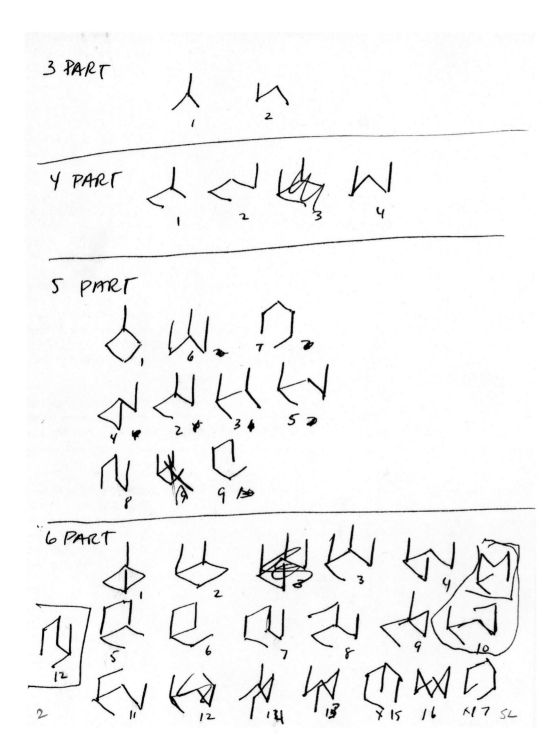

3 PART

4 PART

5 PART

6 PART

Miller-Keller for their thoughtful and detailed comments on my essay. Thanks also to Roger L. Conover and colleagues at MIT Press for their strong commitment to this publication. The high quality of reproductions is largely thanks to John Groo, who dedicated himself to photographing LeWitt's work with great energy and sensitivity. It has been a pleasure to work again with vBureau.com, and in particular Marlene McCarty, who developed the imaginative and stylish design of this book.

Conversations with many friends and colleagues aided in the development of this project. I would like to acknowledge the very helpful contributions of Gabriella De Ferrari, Gary Garrels, David Joselit, Pam Lee, Carol LeWitt, Kazuko Miyamoto, Adrian Piper, and Elizabeth Sussman. Above all, I would like to thank Jonathan Flatley for his engagement with this project, which has ranged far further than the contribution of a remarkable text. Our frequent discussions have added enormously to the pleasures of thinking through the significance of LeWitt's work.

Many of my colleagues at the Wadsworth Atheneum have dedicated themselves to the realization of this exhibition with great enthusiasm. My deep gratitude to those most directly involved: Cecil Adams, Jeremy Barrows, Daphne Deeds, Gretchen Dietrich, Dana DeLoach, Zenon Gansziniec, Mark Giuliano, Janet Heim, Allison Hewey, Susan Hood, Honora Horan, David Kaminski, Stephen Kornhauser, Ann McCrae, Dina Plapler, Linda Roth, Edd Russo, Mary Schroeder, Matthew Siegal, William Staples, John Teahan, Nicole Wholean, and Steve Winot.

The exhibition has been enriched by a significant number of loans from The LeWitt Collection, and I thank Carol and Sol LeWitt for their commitment and boundless generosity. My great thanks to the many other lenders who have contributed important works to the exhibition: Bayly Museum, University of Virginia; Paula Cooper; Douglas S. Cramer; Doris and Donald Fisher; Karla and Walter M. Goldschmidt; Hood Museum of Art, Dartmouth College; Collection Lockhart; Herbert Lust Gallery; Minneapolis Institute of Arts; Sheldon Memorial Art Gallery and Sculpture Garden, University of Nebraska-Lincoln; Joan S. Sonnabend; Weatherspoon Art Gallery, The University of North Carolina at Greensboro; Wexner Center for the Arts, The Ohio State University; and four anonymous lenders.

Our excitement about this exhibition has been shared by colleagues at several distinguished museums. Their collaboration has ensured that the exhibition will reach a wider audience and take on new life at each venue. Particular thanks to Hugh Gourley, Director, Colby College Museum of Art, Maine; Katharine Lee Reid, Director, and Diane De Grazia, Chief Curator, The Cleveland Museum of Art, Ohio; Robert Knight, Director, and Debra Hopkins, Curator of Exhibitions, Scottsdale Museum of Contemporary Art, Arizona.

A special privilege of being the curator of contemporary art at the Wadsworth Atheneum is the opportunity to work closely with Sol LeWitt, whose impressive stature as an artist is matched by his generosity as a collector and patron. Above all, LeWitt believes in art and artists; his own remarkable and prolific career, his commitment to fellow artists and his support of this museum all are natural expressions of this passionate dedication. Sol has supported my research with serene benevolence; he has patiently answered endless questions, looked closely with me at his working drawings and shared his diaries. At the same time, Sol has preserved a rigorous detachment from the project, never seeking to influence my judgments or question my approach. For that extraordinary generosity I remain profoundly grateful.

Nicholas Baume
Emily Hall Tremaine Curator of Contemporary Art

CAT. 2
WORKING DRAWING
FOR INCOMPLETE OPEN CUBES, 1973-74
INK AND PENCIL ON PAPER
7 3/8 X 5 1/2"
THE LEWITT COLLECTION,
CHESTER, CONNECTICUT

12

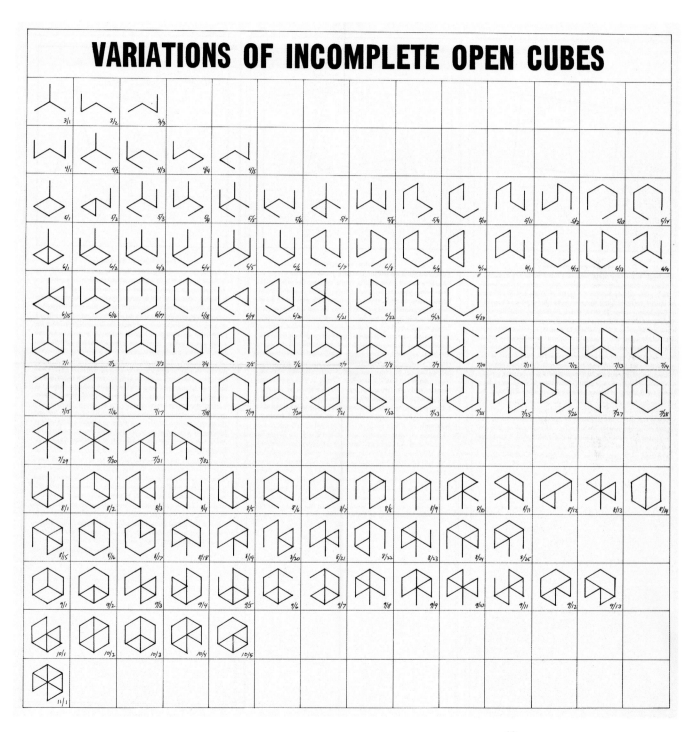

VARIATIONS OF INCOMPLETE OPEN CUBES

INCOMPLETE OPEN CUBES

CAT. 66
COVER FROM
SOL LEWITT: INCOMPLETE OPEN CUBES, 1974
ARTIST'S BOOK, 122 PAGES
JOHN WEBER GALLERY (NEW YORK) 1974
8 X 8 X 5/8"
THE LEWITT COLLECTION,
CHESTER, CONNECTICUT

14

THREE PART VARIATIONS

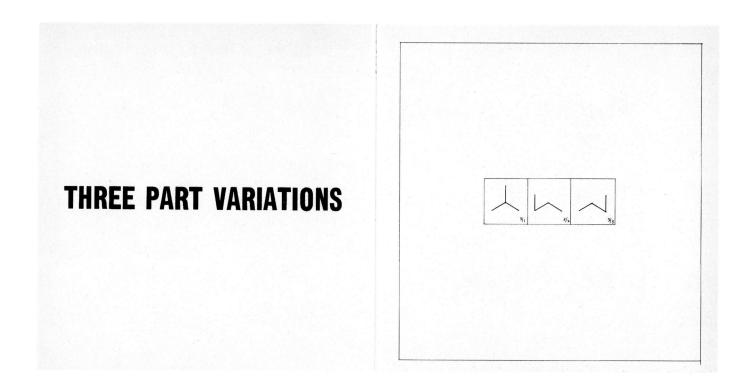

CAT. 66
THREE PART VARIATIONS FROM
SOL LEWITT: INCOMPLETE OPEN CUBES, 1974
ARTIST'S BOOK, 122 PAGES
JOHN WEBER GALLERY (NEW YORK) 1974
8 X 8 X 5/8"
THE LEWITT COLLECTION,
CHESTER, CONNECTICUT

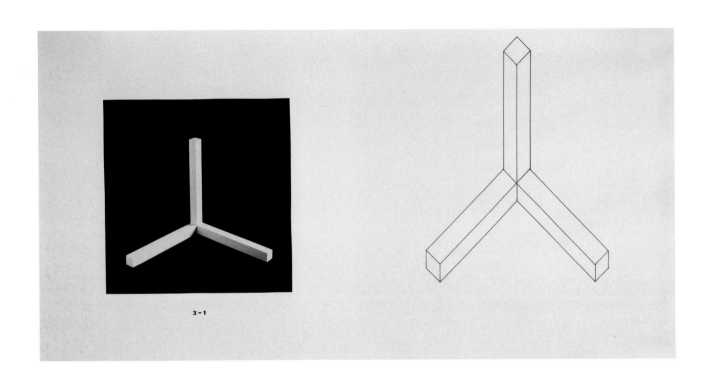

3-1

CAT. 31
INCOMPLETE OPEN CUBE 3/1, 1974
BLACK AND WHITE PHOTOGRAPH, INK AND
PENCIL ON VELLUM
13 X 25"
THE LEWITT COLLECTION,
COURTESY OF THE WADSWORTH ATHENEUM
MUSEUM OF ART, HARTFORD

CAT. 34
INCOMPLETE OPEN CUBE 3/1, 1974
PAINTED ALUMINUM
40 X 40 X 40"
THE LEWITT COLLECTION,
CHESTER, CONNECTICUT

18

CAT. 33
3/2 FROM
*SCHEMATIC DRAWINGS FOR
INCOMPLETE OPEN CUBES, 1974*
INK AND PENCIL ON VELLUM
131 PARTS
12 X 12" EACH
THE LEWITT COLLECTION,
CHESTER, CONNECTICUT

3/2

S. LeWitt

19

THE MUSIC OF FORGETTING

NICHOLAS BAUME

I DO NOT KNOW OF ANY MORE PROFOUND DIFFERENCE IN THE WHOLE ORIENTATION OF AN ARTIST THAN THIS, WHETHER HE LOOKS AT HIS WORK IN PROGRESS (AT "HIMSELF") FROM THE POINT OF VIEW OF THE WITNESS, OR WHETHER HE "HAS FORGOTTEN THE WORLD," WHICH IS THE ESSENTIAL FEATURE OF ALL MONOLOGICAL ART; IT IS BASED ON FORGETTING, IT IS THE MUSIC OF FORGETTING.

FRIEDRICH NIETZSCHE [1]

The music of forgetting is a particularly apt metaphor for the art of Sol LeWitt. The phrase combines in a surprising way two apparently antithetical ideas, both of which are suggestive in relation to LeWitt. Music, the most abstract artistic form, can transport us through its unfolding internal logic to a place of intellectual and emotional reverie. Forgetting, as the psychic act of negation, can clear the mind in order to make space in which to think anew. Like Nietzsche's music of forgetting, LeWitt's art combines to striking effect seemingly incompatible elements. Moreover, it too represents the paradoxical experience of an aesthetic affirmation generated through negation.

Sol LeWitt's conceptualism is a powerful methodology of forgetting. It came into being as an answer to the creative paralysis induced by the triumph and subsequent enervation of American Abstract Expressionism. In order to make art new, its history had to be actively "forgotten." Forgetting, in this sense, is not a literal amnesia, but an affirmative strategy to overcome the burden of history. The belief that one's work was reinventing art by returning to ground zero has been one of the most productive fictions in twentieth century art. The conceptual approach gave LeWitt, whose ambitions exceeded those of second generation Abstract Expressionism, the permission he needed to make things again; to remove all self-censorship in the "perfunctory" execution of "art ideas." No more transcendent self-expression. Painting and sculpture were banished, along with their historical baggage, to be replaced by "structures" and "wall drawings."

LeWitt's conceptualism demanded total immersion in the procedures, progressions and systems that establish autonomous rules of artistic operation with resolute indifference to the world at large. "Irrational thoughts," he declared, "should be followed absolutely and logically." [2] Unlike the parallel tradition of Pop Art, LeWitt's conceptualist pursuit of autonomy insisted on the forgetting of objects and images in the world: "Obviously a drawing of a person is not a real person, but a drawing of a line is a real line." [3] As this observation suggests,

and as will be seen in relation to *Variations of Incomplete Open Cubes*, LeWitt's stance is also an anti-metaphysical one.

In the conceptualist model, subjective expression was replaced by objective thought; a reorientation of art from form to content, from the visual to the conceptual. LeWitt's *Variations of Incomplete Open Cubes* brings to a climax, and expresses in its most sophisticated and elaborate form, the approach to art-making that has made LeWitt one of the most influential artists of his generation. No other serial project by LeWitt embodies with such eloquence so many of the central artistic concerns of the period. Above all, *Incomplete Open Cubes* exemplifies the astonishingly fecund deployment of a single idea to become "a machine that makes the art." [4]

LeWitt's writings of the late 1960s are the most articulate methodological statement issued by any artist of his generation. Critic Peter Schjeldahl recently observed that LeWitt's "Sentences on Conceptual Art" "may be the most concisely resonant and weirdly practical text of aesthetic philosophy since Aristotle." [5] It might seem paradoxical, then, that LeWitt is also the least ideologically fixed of artists in relation to the interpretation of his own work. LeWitt: "The artist may not necessarily understand his own art. His perception is neither better nor worse than that of others." [6]

Interpreting LeWitt's work is, nevertheless, a tricky business. For an artist of his seminal importance, there has been relatively little theorization of his work and its implications since the late 1970s. Perhaps the eloquence of LeWitt's own writings has at once defined and foreclosed the field. Another significant factor, as we shall see, may be that every critical position on the work seems also to imply its opposite – for which a reasonable case can generally be made. This points to the

1.
Friedrich Nietzsche, "The first distinction to be made regarding works of art," aphorism no. 367, *The Gay Science*, trans. Walter Kaufmann (New York: Vintage Books, 1974), p. 324.
2.
Sol LeWitt, "Sentences on Conceptual Art," in *Sol LeWitt: Critical Texts* (hereafter *SLCT*), ed. Adachiara Zevi (Rome: I Libri di AEIOU, 1994), p.88; originally published in *Art-Language* 1, no. 1 (May 1969).
3.
Sol LeWitt, "Sol LeWitt Interviewed," interview by Andrew Wilson, in *SLCT*, p. 125; originally published in *Art Monthly* (London), no. 164 (March 1993).
4.
Sol LeWitt, "Paragraphs on Conceptual Art," in *SLCT*, p. 78; originally published in *Artforum* (New York) 5, no. 10 (June 1967).
5.
Peter Schjeldahl, "Less is Beautiful," *The New Yorker* (March 13, 2000): p.99.
6.
LeWitt, "Sentences on Conceptual Art," in *SLCT*, p. 90.

fact that the work is fundamentally paradoxical, that it resists fixity of meaning, and that its strength lies in its very ability simultaneously to animate contradictory ideas.

7.
LeWitt, "Paragraphs on Conceptual Art," in *SLCT*, p. 80.
8.
Donald Kuspit, "Sol LeWitt: The Look of Thought," in *SLCT*, pp. 209-225; originally published in *Art in America* (New York) 63, no. 5 (Sept. — Oct. 1975).
9.
Kuspit, in *SLCT*, pp. 222-3.
10.
Ibid., p. 213.
11.
Ibid., p. 212.
12.
Ibid., p. 215.
13.
Ibid., p. 220.
14.
Joseph Masheck, "Kuspit's LeWitt: Has He Got Style?," in *SLCT*, pp. 226-236; originally published in *Art in America* (New York) 64, no. 6 (Nov. — Dec. 1976).
15.
Masheck, in *SLCT*, p. 233.
16.
Rosalind Krauss, "LeWitt in Progress," in *SLCT*, pp. 239-249; originally published in *October* 6 (fall 1978): pp. 47-60.
17.
Krauss, in *SLCT*, p. 240.
18.
Ibid., p. 244. Robert Smithson, who had perceptively written of LeWitt, "His concepts are prisons devoid of reason," anticipated Krauss's reading in 1968, in Robert Smithson, "A Museum of Language in the Vicinity of Art," in *Minimalism*, ed. James Meyer (London: Phaidon, 2000), p. 240; originally published in *Art International* (March 1968): pp. 67-78
19.
Krauss, in *SLCT*, "LeWitt in Progress," p. 247.

The intention of this publication and accompanying exhibition is to look in depth at *Variations of Incomplete Open Cubes*, a single but expansive project, finding in it both a characteristic example of LeWitt's artistic process and a case study in conceptualism. With the benefit of historical distance, it also seems possible to consider aspects of the work played down at its inception. This essay examines the powerful sensual appeal of the work; the fascination in LeWitt's detailed working drawings; the overwhelming visual stimulation of all 122 variations presented in three dimensions; the serene stasis of the schematic drawings juxtaposed with the ideographic singularity of the black-and-white photographs; and, finally, the sheer physical presence of the large scale variations. The following discussion begins with a summary of competing critical positions related to *Incomplete Open Cubes*, and continues with an exploration of the project's immanent logic and its relationship to LeWitt's principal themes.

IT DOESN'T REALLY MATTER IF THE VIEWER UNDERSTANDS THE CONCEPTS OF THE ARTIST BY SEEING THE ART. ONCE IT IS OUT OF HIS HAND THE ARTIST HAS NO CONTROL OVER THE WAY A VIEWER WILL PERCEIVE THE WORK. DIFFERENT PEOPLE WILL UNDERSTAND THE SAME THING IN A DIFFERENT WAY. SOL LEWITT [7]

The consensus among art historians and critics is that *Variations of Incomplete Open Cubes* is one of LeWitt's most important works. Yet it is also the work through which the most dramatic schism in interpretation develops. The key positions in this debate were taken well over twenty years ago, when the art historical dust had barely settled on LeWitt's forms.

Although many critics had written about LeWitt's work, the most extreme articulation of what could be termed the "rationalist" interpretation was that of Donald Kuspit in his essay, "Sol LeWitt: The Look of Thought," [8] written in response to the exhibition "Wall Drawings and Structures: The

Location of Six Geometric Figures / Variations of Incomplete Open Cubes" at the John Weber Gallery, New York, in October 1974. Kuspit argues that LeWitt responds to a crisis of meaning in art: "the abnormality of making privileged objects in a scientific–technological civilization." [9] LeWitt, he argues, "is a traditionalist in that he is in search of a universal meaning of art. Rather than contributing to the anarchy of contemporary art by creating still another style, he bends his objects under the yoke of mathematical order to imply a universal meaning." [10] And, for Kuspit, that universal meaning is "that order in and for itself is the essence of art, and is a general condition for its meaning." [11] Kuspit acknowledges, however, that "the incomplete open cubes lose rather than gain formal clarity through their proliferating redundancy." [12] The result of this, nevertheless, is that "it is an ideal of meaning that is emphasized, not a literal unity." [13] That ideal is the complete cube, Kuspit suggests, insofar as it is an abstraction of order itself.

A direct response came from Joseph Masheck in, "Kuspit's LeWitt: Has He Got Style?" [14] Masheck takes exception to Kuspit's characterization of LeWitt's work as "styleless," describing it instead as being in dialogue with art historical styles from classicism to constructivism. While Masheck is dubious of Kuspit's claims for LeWitt's objects as "stepping-stones to the universal idea of art," [15] he does not dispute his basic rationalist interpretation. A more fundamental attack, however, appeared in Rosalind Krauss's essay, "LeWitt in Progress," which argues that *Incomplete Open Cubes* is, in fact, a parody of rationality. [16]

With reference to the criticism of Kuspit, Lucy Lippard, Suzi Gablick and others, Krauss observes, "For almost no writer who deals with LeWitt is there any question that these geometric emblems are the illustration of Mind, the demonstration of rationalism itself." [17] Krauss counters this received view with an analysis of LeWitt's process as obsessional, viewing his rambling serial expansion as the opposite of logical thought: "The experience of the work goes exactly counter to 'the look of thought,' particularly if thought is understood as classical expressions of logic. For such expressions, whether diagrammatic or symbolic, are precisely about the capacity to abbreviate, to adumbrate, to condense, to be able to imply an expansion with only the first two or three terms…" [18]

Krauss finds in *Incomplete Open Cubes*, "The aesthetic manipulations of an absurdist nominalism." [19] In other words, she believes that LeWitt's art is based on a world view that is skeptical of any claims to universal truths or transcendental ideas. Indeed, Krauss finds this attitude to be characteristic of many artists and writers of LeWitt's generation. Emphasizing this correspondence, she intersperses her text with extracts from Samuel Beckett's *Molloy*, an absurdist piece in which the protagonist works through a system for sucking stones. The critical acumen and literary brilliance of Krauss's essay make it both a stunning rejection of the "rationalist" position and a compelling argument for the true modernity of LeWitt's art as essentially anti-metaphysical.

For all its rhetorical force, Krauss's interpretation leaves significant questions about the work itself unanswered. Is LeWitt's objective, or the primary effect of the work, confined to "covering over an abyss of irrationality"?[20] Why would he bother to deploy a system to generate forms with an aspiration for them also to be "interesting and exciting"?[21] Krauss focuses her exclusive attention on the group of 122eight-inch variations. She never mentions the schematic drawings, photographs, artist's book or forty-inch versions that are integral to the project. To do so would perhaps have underlined the extent to which LeWitt was interested in the particular experiential qualities of each articulation of the incomplete open cube idea which, we will see, are dramatically different. Krauss's interpretation depends on the work's primary effect being "an experience that is obsessional in kind."[22] Yet this does not adequately describe, for example, our primary experience of the artist's book or of the individual large-scale aluminum variations.

Ultimately, neither the rationalist nor the more insightful nominalist interpretation provides a fully satisfying account of the complexity of LeWitt's work. It is revealing, however, that the work elicits such contradictory responses. It is, in fact, the work's ability to create and sustain a dialogue between contradictory impulses that is most characteristic. It is in the conversation between the rational and the irrational, the objective and the subjective, the identical and the different, the whole and the part, the ordered and the confused, the intuitive and the counter-intuitive, that the meaning of LeWitt's work unfolds.

In terms of the internal development of LeWitt's work, the genesis of *Incomplete Open Cubes* depends on three central themes: the cube, seriality and incompleteness. The first two had preoccupied LeWitt since the 1960s but were taken in this work to a new level of complexity and elaboration. The third theme represents a contrary move in relation to open cubic forms, which had also been central to LeWitt's work since the 1960s. At the same time, "incompleteness" was a new means for LeWitt to explore another of his recurrent themes: the structural implication of objects that cannot be seen by the arrangement of those that can.

Although its form is never explicitly stated, the concept of a complete cube is the prime mover for *Incomplete Open Cubes*. In the 1960s, LeWitt was attracted to the cube as a "grammatical device, from which the work may proceed," finding it "relatively uninteresting" in itself.[24] With *Incomplete Open Cubes*, it might be said that LeWitt finally sets free his inner cubes – all 122 of them. If the cube is so familiar as to be uninteresting and almost invisible, the open cube structures surprise us in their distinctiveness and variety. Among the remarkable antinomies of the project is the fact that different variations look so different and yet are united in their shared "cubeness." Who would have thought that the simple idea of "incomplete open cubes" would yield 122 variations? Certainly not LeWitt, who noted, "at first I thought it was not a complex project."[25]

In the early 1960s, seriality became an important device in the work of LeWitt and other artists of his generation including Dan Flavin, Donald Judd and Mel Bochner. It provided a means to escape the latest evolution in the ideology and rhetoric of romanticism, which had pervaded Abstract Expressionism during the 1950s. For LeWitt, seriality involved "a way of creating art that did not rely on the whim of the moment but on consistently thought out processes that gave results that were interesting and exciting."[26] LeWitt drew inspiration from the work of Edweard Muybridge, whose time-lapse serial photography captured unpredictable and engaging images of human and animal locomotion (FIG. 1). LeWitt's first major three-dimensional

20.
Ibid., p. 245.
21.
Sol LeWitt, "Excerpts from a Correspondence, 1981-1983," correspondence with Andrea Miller-Keller, in *SLCT*, p. 117; originally published in *Sol LeWitt Wall Drawings 1968-1984*, ed. Susanna Singer (Amsterdam: Stedelijk Museum; Eindhoven: Van Abbemuseum; Hartford: Wadsworth Atheneum; 1984).
22.
Krauss, in *SLCT*, "LeWitt in Progress," p. 244.
23.
Sol LeWitt, "A Conversation with Gary Garrels," interview by Gary Garrels, in *Open: Magazine of the San Francisco Museum of Modern Art*, no.1, (winter/spring 2000): p. 35.
24.
Sol LeWitt, "The Cube," in *SLCT*, p.72; originally published in *Art in America*, New York, (summer 1966).
25.
Sol LeWitt, "Commentaries," in *Sol LeWitt*, ed. Alicia Legg (New York: The Museum of Modern Art, 1978), p. 81.
26.
LeWitt, "Excerpts," p. 117.

work in this vein was *Serial Project No. I (ABCD)* (1966) which involved regulated changes to a series of open and closed geometric forms (FIG. 2). In its execution, *Variations of Incomplete Open Cubes* is LeWitt's most complex and elaborated serial project, although its idea is the most simply expressed.

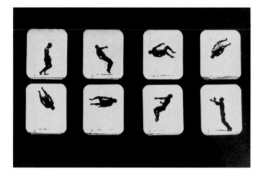

FIG.1 - TOP LEFT

Eadweard Muybridge
The Attitudes of Animals in Motion PLATE 106. Twisting Summersault, 1881
Gelatin silver prints, toned
9 3/4 x 10 7/8"
The LeWitt Collection, Chester, Connecticut

FIG.2 - TOP RIGHT

Sol LeWitt
Serial Project No.1 (ABCD), 1966
Baked enamel on aluminum
Collection of The Museum of Modern Art, New York
Gift of Agnes Gund and purchase (by exchange).

FIG.3 - BOTTOM LEFT

Piet Mondrian
Painting 1, 1926
Collection of The Museum of Modern Art, New York
Katherine S. Dreier Bequest, 1953

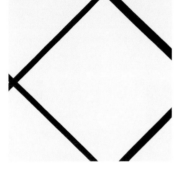

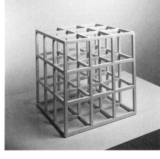

CAT.1

27.
LeWitt, "Commentaries," p. 52.
28.
Sol LeWitt, Serial Project I (ABCD), in *SLCT*, pp. 76-77; originally published in *Aspen* (Aspen), sect. 17, nos. 5 and 6 (1966).
29.
LeWitt, "Paragraphs on Conceptual Art," in *SLCT*, p. 80.
30.
Sol LeWitt, conversation with author and Jonathan Flatley, 9 August 2000.
31.
Sol LeWitt, conversation with author, 4 August 2000.

LeWitt first "opened" his three-dimensional forms in 1964, revealing their skeletal structure. He soon began to experiment with grid-based modular progressions of the basic element, the cube (CAT. 1, PAGE 6). By 1973, having explored this essentially additive process in detail, LeWitt turned to the idea of subtraction. What could be made by taking this modular form, the 12-part open cube, and subtracting each of its parts in a systematic way? It should be noted that while *Incomplete Open Cubes* is subtractive in terms of LeWitt's methodology, it is presented as an incremental accumulation, starting at the three-part, and adding elements up to the eleven-part variations. Again, LeWitt orchestrates a conversation between opposites.

For LeWitt, "the idea of inferring the unknown by clues from the known"[27] had been important since the early 1960s. In *Serial Project I (ABCD)*, the system results in the placement of some forms inside other forms. LeWitt notes, "If the viewer cannot see the interior form, one may believe it is there or not, but one knows which form one believes is there or not there. The evidence given him or her by the other pieces is the set, and by reference to the other sets will inform the viewer as to what should be there."[28] *Incomplete Open Cubes* shifts the emphasis from concealment to making a part suggest the whole. This was not a new idea in abstract art, as can be seen in the work of Mondrian – to take one typologically related example (FIG. 3). LeWitt, however, takes the notion to a more conceptual level, where the idea of the cube must be understood *a priori* if its "missing" parts are to be mentally reconstructed by the viewer.

IF THE ARTIST CARRIES THROUGH HIS IDEA AND MAKES IT INTO VISIBLE FORM, THEN ALL THE STEPS IN THE PROCESS ARE OF IMPORTANCE. THE IDEA ITSELF, EVEN IF NOT MADE VISUAL, IS AS MUCH A WORK OF ART AS ANY FINISHED PRODUCT. ALL INTERVENING STEPS—SCRIBBLES, SKETCHES, DRAWINGS, FAILED WORKS, MODELS, STUDIES, THOUGHTS, CONVERSATIONS—ARE OF INTEREST. THOSE THAT SHOW THE THOUGHT PROCESS OF THE ARTIST ARE SOMETIMES MORE INTERESTING THAN THE FINAL PRODUCT. SOL LEWITT [29]

In the case of *Incomplete Open Cubes*, the "intervening steps" do not upstage the "final product", but they are of considerable interest as remarkable documents that attest to the fearsome complexity of the seemingly simple task LeWitt set himself.[30] LeWitt recalls that he began to work on the project in 1973 and probably had the bulk of it figured out by the end of that year.[31] This is confirmed by LeWitt's diary, which notes the execution of 12 x 12" schematic drawings – which are a final stage in the project - beginning in mid-January of 1974. Most of the working drawings, of which over 50 remain in LeWitt's archive, probably date from 1973, and reflect different stages in the evolution of his thinking. They range from rough freehand sketches to more precise and systematic notations.

The more elaborated drawings chart LeWitt's "failed" attempts to find a systematic means of figuring out the exact number and form of possible variations on paper. The first system involved assigning letters to each of the eight corners of a complete cube. Twelve lines (or parts) connect the eight corners, forming a cube. The parameters LeWitt set for the project include the implication of a three-dimensional cube –

hence one- or two-part variations were ineligible – and no repetitions of identical forms. The difference between a mirror image, which is not identical, and a repetition rotated so that it appears to be different, is often difficult to discern. Many of LeWitt's rough sketches were an effort to work through the problems of rotation and sequence (CAT. 2+3, PAGES 12+10). It became critically important for him to find a systematic way of identifying and eliminating variations that were repetitions of the same form merely rotated.

LeWitt attempted to identify the variations by working through all possible combinations of a specified number of connecting letters. The three- and four-part variations proved relatively simple to identify (CAT. 12). However, the degree of difficulty - and room for error – grew exponentially as the number of parts increased up to seven. While using the letter system, LeWitt initially identified 39 seven-part variations, when in fact there are 32 (CAT. 14, PAGE 59). After seven, the number of possible variations decreases again, concluding with only one of 11 parts.

LeWitt then supplanted the alphabetical system with a numerical one. Again, a complete open cube provided the template, this time with each of its 12 parts numbered separately. This shift enabled LeWitt to introduce a further attempt to systematize the process by working out complementary pairs and mirror images at the same time. For example, he could work on four- and eight-part, or five- and seven-part combinations (CAT. 22, PAGE 32). In taking this approach, LeWitt posited every variation of the parts, even those which would float unattached in space and hence be impossible. He thus found a permutational system that could, in theory, ensure that no variations were overlooked, while at the same time being able to figure out two or more variations at once. What it still lacked, however, was a means of identifying repetitions. LeWitt recalls, "I was trying to figure out a way to do it through numbers or letters logically, but in the end it all had to be done empirically. I had to build a model for each one and then rotate it."[32] This observation pinpoints the moment at which the process of elaboration moved beyond normal human perceptual capacity. Referring to his own practice, sculptor Tony Smith reached a similar conclusion: "We think in two dimensions – horizontally and vertically. Any angle off that is hard to remember. For that reason I make models – drawings would be impossible."[33]

LeWitt's roughest models were made from bent paper clips and pipe cleaners, followed by more elaborate 4-inch versions

CAT. 2

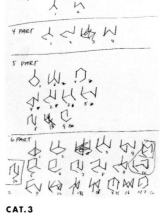

CAT. 3

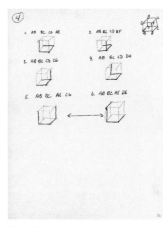

CAT. 12

CAT. 14

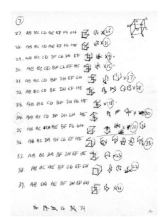

CAT. 22

32.
Ibid.

33.
Tony Smith, "Talking with Tony Smith," interview by Samuel J. Wagstaff,
in *Minimal Art: A Critical Anthology*, ed. Gregory Battcock, (Los Angeles:
University of California Press, 1995), p. 385.

34.
LeWitt, conversation, 4 August 2000.

35.
For example, line drawings of various cubes appear on March 4 — 7, with the
notation: "Balsa 4 x 4 x 4."

36.
Ibid.

37.
Ibid.

38.
Ibid.

39.
The only exception is 11/1, which is the single variation with 11 parts.

40.
LeWitt, conversation, 9 August 2000.

41.
This was done by two mathematicians, Dr Erna Herrey and Arthur
Babakhanian. LeWitt had originally overlooked a number of variations in his
1967 serial work, *All Three-Part Variations of Different Kinds of Cubes.*
Perhaps he wanted to avoid any similar oversight. He need not have worried,
as his exhaustive empirical process had assured the accuracy of his conclusions. It is worth noting, however, that LeWitt refrained this time from append-
ing "all" to his full title, *Variations of Incomplete Open Cubes.* When recently
asked what he would do if a new variation was found, LeWitt replied with the
irony of an artist who has never been concerned with the marketing of his
work, "That would be good news. I hear they're selling very well!" in LeWitt,
conversation, 9 August 2000.

42.
Sol LeWitt, conversation with author, 9 September 2000.

43.
Sol LeWitt, public discussion with Gary Garrels and Andrea Miller-Keller, San
Francisco Museum of Modern Art, 19 February 2000.

44.
LeWitt, "A Conversation with Gary Garrels," p. 30.

CAT.48

in balsa wood. These models do not appear to have survived – some may have been given to fabricators to assist in making the 40-inch versions.[34] LeWitt's 1974 diary notes the construction of balsa models in late February and early March.[35] It is clear that by this point, the series was already close to its final form.

In addition to there being no systematic way to work out the variations on paper, there also proved to be no consistent way to arrange the cubes within their numbered sub-groupings. If we look again at the alphabetical working drawing for the 7-part variations (cat. 14), it suggests that the first 9 variations contain one complete side, which is oriented to the ground. This makes intuitive sense as the complete side may then function as a base, the repetition of which makes it easier to follow the variations. In the final work, however, only the first variation, 7/1, ends up with a complete side on the ground. All the others with one or more complete side are rotated to different planes. One effect of this is to make the sequence of cubes difficult to follow. Confusion, however, was not his intention. In fact, he wanted to present the work as clearly as possible: "When I finally figured it out, I wanted to show it so it explains itself the best way. The book was one way, the three-dimensional structures were another, and the schematic drawings were another."[36] Why, then, are many of the variations presented in rotations that appear counter-intuitive?

LeWitt resists any suggestion that this was an aesthetic decision. The answer, he recalls, is that he simply wanted to reduce the number of elements floating unsupported in space in order to minimize mechanical strain on the joints and enhance stability. This seems a credible explanation and is in keeping with LeWitt's tendency to find consistent principles of organization even if an all-encompassing system is impossible. It was not possible, for example, to eliminate all the unsupported horizontal elements. Nor was it possible to increase the stability of every variation; 6/24 (cat. 48) is inherently unstable regardless of its rotation. Stability, notes LeWitt, "wasn't the final determinant. I had to do all the work. Some of them were more precarious than others, but I wouldn't reject it because of that."[37] However arrived at, the consequences of LeWitt's placement

decisions are, of course, aesthetic. Had he consistently left a complete side oriented to the ground, that side would have functioned as a conventional base. It would also have reduced the overall number of parts projecting from the ground plane into space. These two effects would have made the presentation more static and repetitive, and less suggestive of the three-dimensional space of the cube. In the final work, the rotation of the cubes often seems surprising and even whimsical. The overall impression produces a kind of system-effect; the appearance of a logic that is nevertheless inscrutable.

Within the sub-groups of variations, each is numbered based on how many parts it has and where it falls in the sequence. As has been seen in regard to rotation, the sequence is not based on an all-inclusive system. LeWitt recalls, "There was no systematic way of doing it, although I tried to start at the simplest and work toward the more complicated."[38] Once again, despite the lack of a total system, there are consistent principles of organization. The first variation in each group is symmetrical and therefore has no mirror-image variation.[39] As LeWitt put it: "The first one has no brother. The other ones have brothers and sisters, so they're grouped together."[40] It seems reasonable to conclude, then, that the placement and sequence were dictated by a number of overlapping organizational principles, all mediated by the artist's subjective judgment.

Following the complex process of figuring on paper and testing with models,[41] LeWitt ultimately had his conclusions verified mathematically. They were found to be accurate. LeWitt's process begs the question of why he didn't go first to a mathematician and save himself the trouble of working it out. LeWitt replies: "In the first place, I thought it'd be so easy that it wouldn't be necessary. Secondly, I didn't know any mathematician to ask. Thirdly, it was a kind of challenge to be able to do it and to work it all out. It got to be a game or a puzzle that I wanted to solve."[42] For a conceptualist, the process of working through an idea is as important as the resulting work. LeWitt recently said, "I don't want to deal with any idea so complex that I can't figure it out myself."[43] It is also clear that total immersion in the process is, for LeWitt, one of the pleasures of making art. It is in this process that the world is forgotten and that the artist's ideas, good or bad, are given a chance to take shape: "Sometimes I pick up a bad idea that I've discarded and figure out a different way of doing it, and it may turn out good. My process is just to do them and not to be self-critical, not to second-guess myself; just to do them objectively and not subjectively."[44]

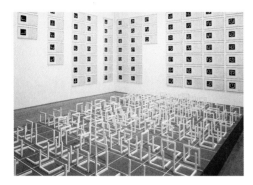

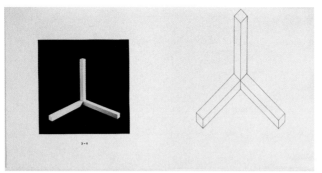

CAT.31

FIG.4 FAR LEFT

Sol LeWitt
Incomplete Open Cubes, 1974
Installation view,
San Francisco Museum of Art
122 painted wood structures on
a painted wooden base and 122
framed photographs and drawings
on paper
Each structure: 8 x 8 x 8"
Base: 12 x 120 x 216"
Each framed element: 14 x 26"
Collection of San Francisco
Museum of Modern Art,
Accessions Committee Fund

CAT.6

SINCE NO FORM IS INTRINSICALLY SUPERIOR TO ANOTHER, THE ARTIST MAY USE ANY FORM, FROM AN EXPRESSION OF WORDS (WRITTEN OR SPOKEN) TO PHYSICAL REALITY, EQUALLY. SOL LEWITT [45]

LeWitt chose to realize the finished work in a number of different forms. Structures eight inches to a side representing the entire series were made in wood, painted white. These, in combination with paired photographs and drawings of each variation, became one work representing the total series (FIG. 4). Forty-inch three-dimensional versions in painted aluminum were also made of all variations, although these were fabricated in different locations over several years. Black-and-white photographs were made of each eight-inch three-dimensional variation. The objects are starkly presented against a black background, eliminating shadows. They are shot from slightly above on either the diagonal axis or, more often, from an oblique angle so as to avoid the confusion of overlapping verticals. As photographed, the scale of the objects is impossible to determine, but the views simulate a natural human point of view were the objects full-scale. LeWitt originally intended to make 122 individual sets, each combining an eight-inch variation, a photograph and a drawing. At least one set was made for variation 3/1 (CAT. 31, PAGE 16). A further 2 5/8-inch three-dimensional painted wood version of the entire series was made in 1982 (CAT. 64, PAGE 2).

Using isometric projection, LeWitt also made individual drawings of each cube viewed axially on translucent vellum. The choice of an isometric view, the most familiar mode of stereometric and mechanical drawing, is consistent with his aim of providing objective visual information: "It explained the piece better than a perspective rendering. The difference is that it wasn't a rendering of the piece, it was a building of the piece using line, so as to understand how it came together in an engineering sense."[46] He made a summary drawing for each sub-group of variations using a simplified,

VARIATIONS OF INCOMPLETE OPEN CUBES

CAT.33   CAT.65   CAT.66

INCOMPLETE OPEN CUBES

linear isometric projection (CAT. 33, PAGE 81). A composite image including all 122 variations in their numerical groupings summarizes the entire series (CAT. 65, PAGE 13). This image was used for the announcement of the first exhibition of the series at John Weber Gallery and as the frontispiece of the book LeWitt made of the project (CAT. 66, PAGE 14). LeWitt used this shorthand method of drawing the cubes while figuring them out (CAT.6). The representation of all 122 variations in a single drawing is an extraordinarily economical and elegant statement of the

45.
LeWitt, "Sentences on Conceptual Art," in *SLCT*, p. 89.
46.
LeWitt, conversation, 9 September 2000.

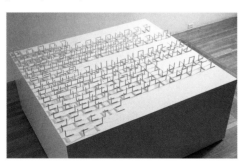

CAT.64

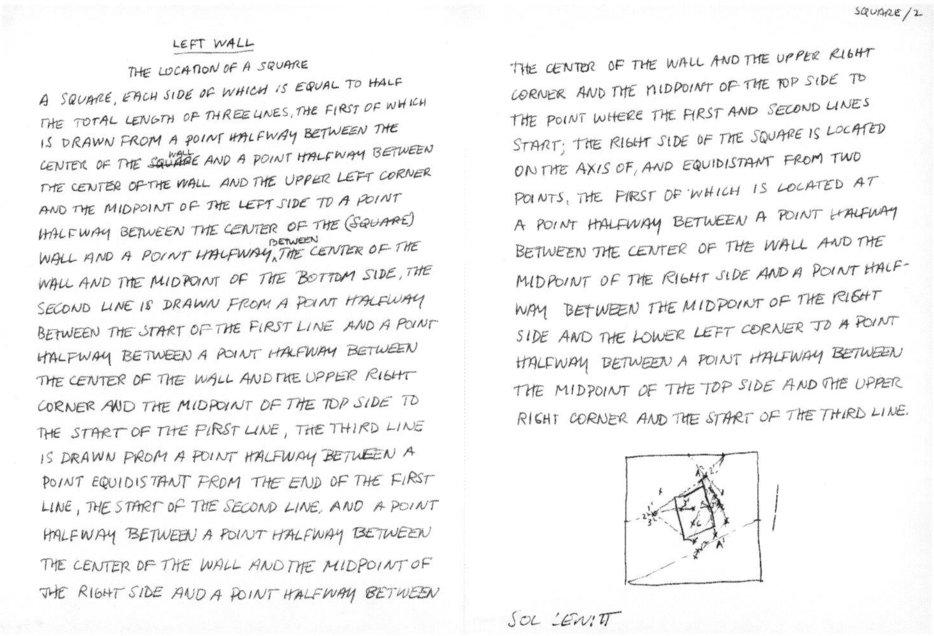

LEFT WALL

THE LOCATION OF A SQUARE

A SQUARE, EACH SIDE OF WHICH IS EQUAL TO HALF THE TOTAL LENGTH OF THREE LINES, THE FIRST OF WHICH IS DRAWN FROM A POINT HALFWAY BETWEEN THE CENTER OF THE SQUARE AND A POINT HALFWAY BETWEEN THE CENTER OF THE WALL AND THE UPPER LEFT CORNER AND THE MIDPOINT OF THE LEFT SIDE TO A POINT HALFWAY BETWEEN THE CENTER OF THE (SQUARE) WALL AND A POINT HALFWAY, BETWEEN THE CENTER OF THE WALL AND THE MIDPOINT OF THE BOTTOM SIDE, THE SECOND LINE IS DRAWN FROM A POINT HALFWAY BETWEEN THE START OF THE FIRST LINE AND A POINT HALFWAY BETWEEN A POINT HALFWAY BETWEEN THE CENTER OF THE WALL AND THE UPPER RIGHT CORNER AND THE MIDPOINT OF THE TOP SIDE TO THE START OF THE FIRST LINE, THE THIRD LINE IS DRAWN FROM A POINT HALFWAY BETWEEN A POINT EQUIDISTANT FROM THE END OF THE FIRST LINE, THE START OF THE SECOND LINE, AND A POINT HALFWAY BETWEEN A POINT HALFWAY BETWEEN THE CENTER OF THE WALL AND THE MIDPOINT OF THE RIGHT SIDE AND A POINT HALFWAY BETWEEN

THE CENTER OF THE WALL AND THE UPPER RIGHT CORNER AND THE MIDPOINT OF THE TOP SIDE TO THE POINT WHERE THE FIRST AND SECOND LINES START; THE RIGHT SIDE OF THE SQUARE IS LOCATED ON THE AXIS OF, AND EQUIDISTANT FROM TWO POINTS, THE FIRST OF WHICH IS LOCATED AT A POINT HALFWAY BETWEEN A POINT HALFWAY BETWEEN THE CENTER OF THE WALL AND THE MIDPOINT OF THE RIGHT SIDE AND A POINT HALFWAY BETWEEN THE MIDPOINT OF THE RIGHT SIDE AND THE LOWER LEFT CORNER TO A POINT HALFWAY BETWEEN A POINT HALFWAY BETWEEN THE MIDPOINT OF THE TOP SIDE AND THE UPPER RIGHT CORNER AND THE START OF THE THIRD LINE.

SOL LEWITT

FIG. 5

Sol LeWitt
The Location of a Square, 1974
Ink on paper
11 x 17"
The LeWitt Collection, Chester, Connecticut

47.
LeWitt, "Sentences on Conceptual Art," in *SLCT*, p. 89.
48.
LeWitt, conversation, 9 August 2000.
49.
Conceiving and entitling works of art "Variations" is more common to music than to visual art — a point further explored in Pamela Lee's *Phase Piece* in this publication.
50.
Another body of work from the same year, *Squares With Sides and Corners Torn Off*, can be seen as related, but different. LeWitt: "Tearing is still a positive action. *Incomplete Open Cubes* is a challenge to find all the ways of not doing something — of doing everything else but completing the cube," in Sol LeWitt, conversation, 9 September, 2000.
51.
For example, noted on 3 April: "sent 4 semi-cube drawings to Bonomo," with an accompanying sketch of the four variations.

IF WORDS ARE USED, AND THEY PROCEED FROM IDEAS ABOUT ART, THEN THEY ARE ART AND NOT LITERATURE; NUMBERS ARE NOT MATHEMATICS. SOL LEWITT **47**

Having found a variety of ways to present the work visually, LeWitt had also to find a suitable way to express it verbally.

entire series. The whole idea is laid out, simply put and seems graspable at a glance. The drawing implies the orderly, systematic elaboration of the idea, starting from three three-part variations and ending in a single one of eleven parts. It is only when we look closer, attempting to discover the pattern of elaboration, the logic of the sequence, or to mentally reconstruct these schematic notations in three dimensions that we become utterly confounded and confused. Yet, at the same time, in the mechanical drawings and artist's book each variation is described visually with the clarity and exactitude of an engineer. This continual exchange between the rational and the irrational is confirmed as a principal dynamic in the work.

He has always favored descriptive titles over the ubiquitous "untitled." Moreover, LeWitt has been interested in using language as integral to his art. He recalls, "The main idea – outside of figuring out all this stuff – was how things can be perceived in different ways. It was about transmitting an idea in different ways though visual means, but also verbally, because there was a title, and it was *Variations of Incomplete Open Cubes*. All are different aspects of communication." **48** LeWitt's title uses familiar descriptive terms, but in a way that remains highly specific to his own practice and methodology. Open cube structures have been, as we have already seen, signature elements in LeWitt's work since the early 1960s. Systematic variations are also featured in previous works.**49** The idea of "incompletion," however, is particular to this work.**50**

The eventual title of the work does not appear in any of LeWitt's working drawings or notes. In his 1974 diary and at least one schematic drawing, the project is simply referred to as "semi-cubes."**51** The prefix "semi" seems possible as a description because it does imply partiality (usually half), but it does not convey a definitive absence as does "incomplete." LeWitt's eventual title thus foregrounds the implicit but unstated idea of the complete cube, from which all variations are derived. This may be true in terms of LeWitt's methodology, but it is not necessarily the way we experience the piece. To make an experiential analogy from nature, when we see the moon in its first phase, we do not think of it first and foremost as incomplete. We refer to it, rather, as a new moon. LeWitt's language thus enacts a kind of de-familiarization of the apparently familiar, just as the variations of this unsurprising object, the cube, startle us in their multiplicity.

Variations of Incomplete Open Cubes is less a naming of the piece than a parallel operation, condensing into language its paradoxical nature. This linguistic operation was of central importance to LeWitt's concurrent series of "Location" drawings. Just as *Incomplete Open Cubes* maps the complex perceptual experience of three-dimensional space, so the "Location" wall drawings shown at the same time concretize in language and line the elaborate spatial relationships generated by the description of a simple geometric figure. LeWitt's first "Location" drawings are concise descriptions of a line or point. By late 1974, they had become prolix to the point of absurdity (FIG. 5). The two projects are thus linked in both process and realization, based on the conceptualization of simple forms in a complex way in two- and three-dimensional

FIG.6

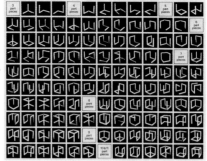

space, all generated relationally. The geometric figures, for example, are generated through relational directions based on the space of their installation, while the different open cubes are generated through relational variations of the open cube form. There is, finally, an ironic touch in LeWitt's title. Had any artist before presented so highly elaborated and "finished" a work as a series of "incomplete" objects?

The articulation of the project in diverse media and different formats extends its conceptual basis by resisting conventional aesthetic hierarchies and demonstrating the generative potential of its basic idea. Although, as we have seen, LeWitt very deliberately arrived at a format for the presentation of the work, he made changes to it depending on the context, and resisted the idea of there being a single "correct" way to show the work. This openness is essential to the idea of "variations." Within the given parameters, there can never be too many different ways to perceive the project and its elements. When the work was first shown in New York, the eight-inch variations were installed on a long narrow table, surrounded by the photograph-drawing diptychs (FIG. 6). The same elements were subsequently shown throughout Europe and the United States in a number of different configurations. By the end of 1976, the project had been shown in Paris, New York, Amsterdam, Edinburgh, Turin, Basel, Cologne, Eindhoven and Geneva. While the numerical groupings and sequence remained consistent, the overall layout and individual orientation changed. This is also true of LeWitt's schematic drawings and composite photographs (CAT. 67, PAGE 8). LeWitt: "For me the layout was entirely open because every time I did it differently. If it was for a publication that had pages that were a different size, then I made it that size." [52]

THE CONVENTIONS OF ART ARE ALTERED BY WORKS OF ART. SOL LEWITT [53]

Our experience of *Incomplete Open Cubes* changes remarkably depending on the form in which it is realized. Not only does LeWitt present us with every systemic variation, but with at least five radically different ways of perceiving each one. Combining linear and solid schematic drawings with photographs, the artist's book reads like a cross between a construction manual and the Rosetta Stone, translating the variations into ideographic characters of near-cuneiform abstraction. Seen in three dimensions, the staccato rhythms of the 2 5/8-inch versions in no way prepare us for the encounter with their imposing 40-inch cousins.

Seven 40-inch variations were shown in the John Weber Gallery exhibition. In contrast to the smaller variations, which together comprise one piece, each large variation is an independent work. In fact, the scale of the project and LeWitt's method of distribution has virtually guaranteed that they will never be seen together. The present exhibition, which assembles roughly a quarter of all the large variations, is the first occasion on which a substantial number have been presented together.

By 1974, LeWitt had numerous dealers in Europe and the United States. He allocated each a number of large variations to fabricate according to his instructions. [54] He also contributed a group to support *Lotte Continua* ("The Continuing Struggle"), a left-wing Italian political organization, and the

52.
LeWitt, conversation, 9 August 2000.
53.
LeWitt, "Sentences on Conceptual Art," in *SLCT*, p. 89.
54.
The works were fabricated using industrial aluminum tubing which varies slightly in size from country to country. This resulted in some marginal differences among overall dimensions, although the proportions are always equal.

radical French newspaper, *Liberation*. LeWitt tabulated this distribution in a number of sketches (CAT. 30).

At 40 inches, these works have a presence related to their human scale. As individual pieces, they can be read more clearly as sculptures and in this sense, more readily absorbed in the conventional terms of three-dimensional art. In this larger scale, the often dramatic compositional effects of each single variation are revealed. The remarkable range in their formal characteristics becomes evident. As one moves around the works, there is a constant play between symmetry and asymmetry, stasis and fluidity, density and openness, clarity and confusion, figuration and abstraction, mirror reflection and inversion. Nevertheless, in conception and execution they are radically different from traditional sculpture in every respect

55.
LeWitt, conversation, 4 August 2000.

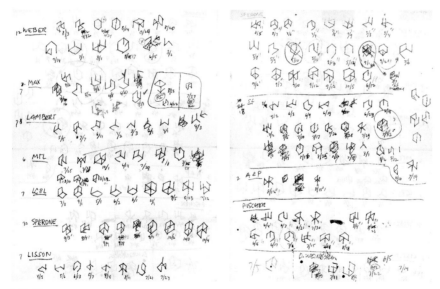

CAT. 30

Whatever the formal attributes of each example and whatever perceptual pleasure can be derived from their contemplation, we cannot escape the fact that each variation has been created through the mechanical implementation of a pre-conceived system in which subjective

"artistic" expression is negated. The work's aesthetic, as well as its process, is machine-like. Each 40-inch variation has been industrially fabricated from standardized aluminum tubing, finished with white enamel. LeWitt counters the conventional fetishization of the unique art object by insisting that these structures are no more than the realization of a concept; if damaged, the work can simply be repainted or remade with no loss of authenticity.

Enlarged and given an independent existence, the aluminum variation operates differently from its smaller counterpart. As a single object it is now mediated by two a priori ideas of totality, the complete cube and the complete series. It is one of 122 variations, all of which have been composed without a conventional creative act of "composition." One cannot be judged superior to another from the perspective of their production – all equally express the idea of the work. This realization sparks another counter-conversation, here contrasting the aesthetic qualities of the object and its non-aesthetic derivation.

There were, of course, many aesthetic choices made by the artist in the creation of *Incomplete Open Cubes*. LeWitt's very decision to invent the system and set its parameters was an aesthetic one. Nevertheless, the self-conscious removal of subjective control from the process of implementation is clear. In those areas of the presentation in which no systematic formulation was possible – the sequence, rotation and overall presentation – LeWitt is ultimately prepared to let the cubes fall where they may. Referring to a 40-inch variation that had been pictured "upside down," LeWitt said: "To me there's no wrong way – it doesn't matter. As long as it's rectilinear, it's okay with me."[55]

As the cube variations come into dialogue with their surroundings in the world at large, including architecture, landscape and people, their distinctiveness is in sharpest relief. The danger of generalizing about the series becomes clear as the differences between, say, a three-part asymmetrical variation and a ten-part symmetrical one are great. So too are the contrasting effects of the same variation situated in different locations. It is here that the "open" nature of the works, both literally and metaphorically, is most evident. A reading of the works as archetypes of modernism is strongest where their formal language is very distinct - in their encounter with nature, or with pre-modernist art and architecture. Yet, in these contexts, LeWitt's work offers not a naively utopian vision of industrial-age perfection, but a poetic meditation on the multiplicity, unpredictability and complexity that exists even within what we conceive of as simple and whole. This is perhaps why *Incomplete Open Cubes* is a quintessential example of LeWitt's particular brand of conceptual art. The general idea of an incomplete open cube can easily be described, but the complex experience of its spatial and contextual relations can only be had through its physical realization. In other words, the system is predetermined but the results of its implementation cannot be imagined by the artist or viewer beforehand. LeWitt reflected on his own pleasure in seeing the results of the project: "I was surprised that they drew such a positive aesthetic reaction – at least from me – and that they would have been unimaginable. Without having seen the actual things, you could never have conjured them up in your mind beforehand."[56]

ISAAC (WOODY ALLEN): ...THE STEEL CUBE WAS BRILLIANT?

MARY (DIANE KEATON): YES. TO ME IT WAS VERY TEXTURAL — YOU KNOW WHAT I MEAN? IT WAS PERFECTLY INTEGRATED AND IT HAD A MARVELOUS KIND OF NEGATIVE CAPABILITY.

— Soho gallery scene, *Manhattan* [57]

LeWitt first chose to work with the cube in the 1960s because he found it the "least emotive"[58] three dimensional form; he chose white "because it was less expressive than black."[59] Nevertheless, both the cube and white do have powerful emotional resonances and expressive effects. LeWitt was not indifferent to this, having observed that "Three-dimensional art of any kind is a physical fact. This physicality is its most obvious expressive content."[60] His conceptualist solution was, "to ameliorate this emphasis on materiality as much as possible or to use it in a paradoxical way (to convert it into an idea)."[61] LeWitt's paradoxical treatment of the form is more thoroughgoing than that of the color. Nevertheless, the repetition of white as the color of nearly all his open structures after 1965 effects a mechanization of aesthetic choice. At the same time, the broader success of LeWitt's art inevitably folds back into the specific materiality of the work a new signification: that of a signature, or even period style. Both the arbitrary nature of LeWitt's use of white and the extent to which it became a signature element in his work of this period are highlighted by an anomalous *Incomplete Open Cube*. When LeWitt found that two examples of the same aluminum variation, 7/8, had been made in error, he had one painted black (FIG. 7). For LeWitt, the resulting piece is just another variation, regardless of how "wrong" it looks relative to the others.

The attributes of materiality cannot be narrowly defined because they depend on changing cultural and historical context and are ultimately subjective. The cube can – as Kuspit would have it – stand for the transcendent power of human reason. This rationalist aesthetic has not been lost on the world of high-tech design and marketing. Witness the latest advertisement for a "cube" computer: "True, it looks like it belongs in the Museum of Modern Art. But the G4 Cube is really a thoroughbred supercomputer that belongs right on your desk." In an entirely different register, it might also stand for mysterious new-age "psychoanalysis." A recent popular publication titled *Secrets of the Cube* asks, "Have you been cubed yet? If you have, you'll find much more here on the meaning of your personal cube."[62]

The other material element of the work, which is at once most ubiquitous and most difficult to pin down, is the color white. LeWitt himself found white to be "apt for contemplation,"[63] and it is easy to recognize its associations with the representation of purity and truth. In contrast, as the traditional color of household appliances, its use over standardized aluminum tubing evokes a techno-modernist aesthetic. White has also often been regarded as the expression of neutrality or absence. Consider the whiteness of the blank page or mythic "tabula rasa," the unpainted canvas, the empty gallery wall. Deconstructive readings, however, have argued that far from signifying an absence of meaning, white is densely layered with symbolic significance. For example, the use of white as an anti-fashion signifier in 20th century architecture was the subject of a recent study which found that it was, in fact, fundamentally fashion-driven. [64]

If whiteness and the cube are vehicles of diversely resonant symbolic meaning, in combination they also represent a particular historical formulation. The "white cube" has long been an archetype of modernist architecture. Derived from the cube, LeWitt's stripped down skeletal variations could be read in reference to the ethical position of anti-decorative modernism, with white the antidote to "criminal" ornamentation, geometry the avatar of function. Yet, the eccentricity of LeWitt's forms undermines any functionalist logic, providing only incidental speculations on a futurist utopia, or perhaps an analogue to the grid-based architectural polyphony of

56.
LeWitt, conversation, 9 September 2000.
57.
Soho gallery scene, Woody Allen, *Manhattan*, 1979.
58.
LeWitt, "The Cube," p. 72.
59.
Sol LeWitt, in "White in Art is White?," *The Print Collector's Newsletter* 8, no. 1, (March-April 1977): p. 2.
60.
LeWitt, "Paragraphs on Conceptual Art," p. 81.
61.
Ibid.
62.
Quoted from an Amazon.com buying information web page (July 2000) for Annie Gottlieb and Slobodan D. Pesic, *Secrets of the Cube: The Ancient Visualization Game That Reveals Your True Self.*
63.
LeWitt, "White in Art is White?," p. 2.
64.
Mark Wigley, *White Walls, Designer Dresses: The Fashioning of Modern Architecture*, The MIT Press, Cambridge and London, 1995. From a different perspective, the symbolic representation of racial whiteness was something Gordon Matta-Clark questioned in 1977: "And can we still deal with white now that *Roots* has made its lasting impression? Can art still have a pure white conscience in the real world?" Gordon Matta-Clark quoted in "White in Art is White?," *The Print Collector's Newsletter*, vol. 8, no. 1, March-April 1977, p. 2.

65.
Brian O'Doherty, *Inside the White Cube: The Ideology of the Gallery Space* (Los Angeles: University of California Press, 1999), p. 79; originally published as a series of essays in *Artforum*, New York, (1976).
66.
LeWitt, "Sentences on Conceptual Art," in *SLCT*, p. 88.

Manhattan itself. The white cube remains, however, synonymous with the modernist space of exhibition. In his 1976 critique, *Inside the White Cube*, Brian O'Doherty observes, "The development of the pristine, placeless white cube is one of modernism's triumphs – a development commercial, esthetic and technological."[65] By association, if not by design, LeWitt's structures may come to represent this moment of modern art's codification and institutionalization.

CONCEPTUAL ARTISTS ARE MYSTICS RATHER THAN RATIONALISTS. THEY LEAP TO CONCLUSIONS THAT LOGIC CANNOT REACH. SOL LEWITT [66]

Sol LeWitt's *Incomplete Open Cubes* might be thought of, both literally and metaphorically, as a kind of "counter intelligence." In the formats in which the entire series is presented, it seems at once to signify meaning and yet, like an unbreakable code, to be impenetrable. In its systematic logic it invites our understanding, yet in its spatial and permutational complexity, it refuses our attempts at comprehending it as a whole. In the formats where we experience the variations individually, we find the unexpected duality of forms that are at once incomplete conceptually and satisfying aesthetically. In every format, the work performs acts of metaphorical counter intelligence, pitting reason against itself, confounding expectations, insisting on paradox.

Perhaps the ultimate paradox is that it is through the negation of subjectivity that LeWitt reaffirms the creative role of the artist. If *Incomplete Open Cubes* negates the romantic approach to making art as the exercise of subjective artistic expression, it does not do so at the expense of the artist. The fact that LeWitt's forms were not the result of an intentional act of creative imagination in the traditional sense does not render the artist obsolete. Instead, LeWitt's conceptualism reinvents at once the methodology and formal language of artistic expression.

Incomplete Open Cubes does not comfort us with intimations of transcendent truth, yet neither does it confine the role of the artist to that of absurdist jester. LeWitt's art presents us with many things, from the complex process of its formulation to the perceptual pleasures and riddles of its apprehension. LeWitt overcomes the unforeseen complications of his "simple" assignment and the trial-and-error confusions of his relentless figuring as he compels his chaos to become form. This aesthetic transformation offers us a case study in mastering the chaos of existence; to contemplate this transformation is to hear the music of LeWitt's forgetting.

CAT. 22
*WORKING DRAWING FOR FIVE- AND SEVEN-
PART INCOMPLETE OPEN CUBES (NUMERICAL),*
1973-74
INK AND PENCIL ON PAPER
1 OF 6 PARTS, 11 X 8 1/2" EACH
THE LEWITT COLLECTION,
CHESTER, CONNECTICUT

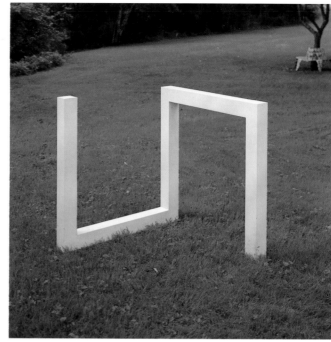

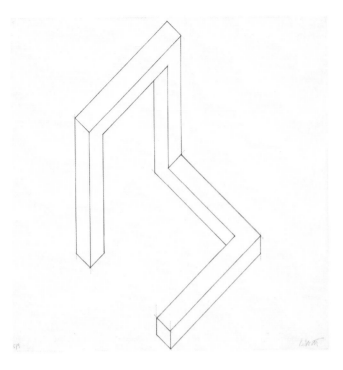

clockwise from top left

CAT. 33
5/9 FROM
SCHEMATIC DRAWINGS FOR
***INCOMPLETE OPEN CUBES*, 1974**
INK AND PENCIL ON VELLUM
131 PARTS
12 X 12" EACH
THE LEWITT COLLECTION,
CHESTER, CONNECTICUT

CAT. 38
***INCOMPLETE OPEN CUBE 5/9*, 1974**
PAINTED ALUMINUM
43 X 43 X 43"
JOAN S. SONNABEND

CAT. 50
***INCOMPLETE OPEN CUBE 7/10*, 1974**
PAINTED ALUMINUM
40 X 40 X 40"
PRIVATE COLLECTION

CAT. 33
7/10 FROM
SCHEMATIC DRAWINGS FOR
***INCOMPLETE OPEN CUBES*, 1974**
INK AND PENCIL ON VELLUM
131 PARTS
12 X 12" EACH
THE LEWITT COLLECTION,
CHESTER, CONNECTICUT

CAT. 36
INCOMPLETE OPEN CUBE 5/2, 1974
PAINTED ALUMINUM
40 X 40 X 40"
THE LEWITT COLLECTION,
CHESTER, CONNECTICUT

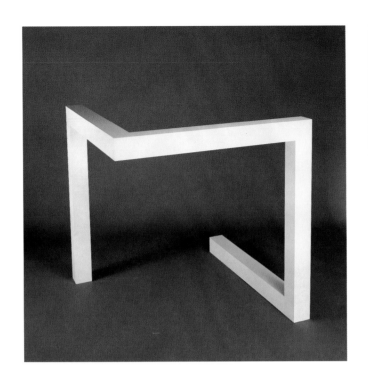 

CAT. 40
INCOMPLETE OPEN CUBE 5/14, 1974
PAINTED ALUMINUM
41 X 41 X 41"
SHELDON MEMORIAL ART GALLERY
AND SCULPTURE GARDEN, UNIVERSITY OF
NEBRASKA-LINCOLN, OLGA N. SHELDON
ACQUISITION TRUST. 1985.U-3744

CAT. 45
INCOMPLETE OPEN CUBE 6/18, 1974
PAINTED ALUMINUM
42 X 42 X 42"
THE LEWITT COLLECTION, COURTESY OF THE
WADSWORTH ATHENEUM MUSEUM OF ART,
HARTFORD

CAT. 47
INCOMPLETE OPEN CUBE 6/23, 1974
PAINTED ALUMINUM
40 X 40 X 40"
THE LEWITT COLLECTION,
CHESTER, CONNECTICUT

CAT. 37
INCOMPLETE OPEN CUBE 5/7, 1974
PAINTED ALUMINUM
40 X 40 X 40"
HERBERT LUST GALLERY

38

CAT. 46
INCOMPLETE OPEN CUBE 6/19, 1974
PAINTED ALUMINUM
40 X 40 X 40"
THE LEWITT COLLECTION,
CHESTER, CONNECTICUT

CAT. 41
INCOMPLETE OPEN CUBE 6/2, 1974
PAINTED ALUMINUM
40 X 40 X 40"
THE LEWITT COLLECTION,
CHESTER, CONNECTICUT

CAT. 43
INCOMPLETE OPEN CUBE 6/9, 1974
PAINTED ALUMINUM
40 X 40 X 40"
THE LEWITT COLLECTION,
CHESTER, CONNECTICUT

CAT. 42
INCOMPLETE OPEN CUBE 6/4, 1974
PAINTED ALUMINUM
40 X 40 X 40"
HERBERT LUST GALLERY

41

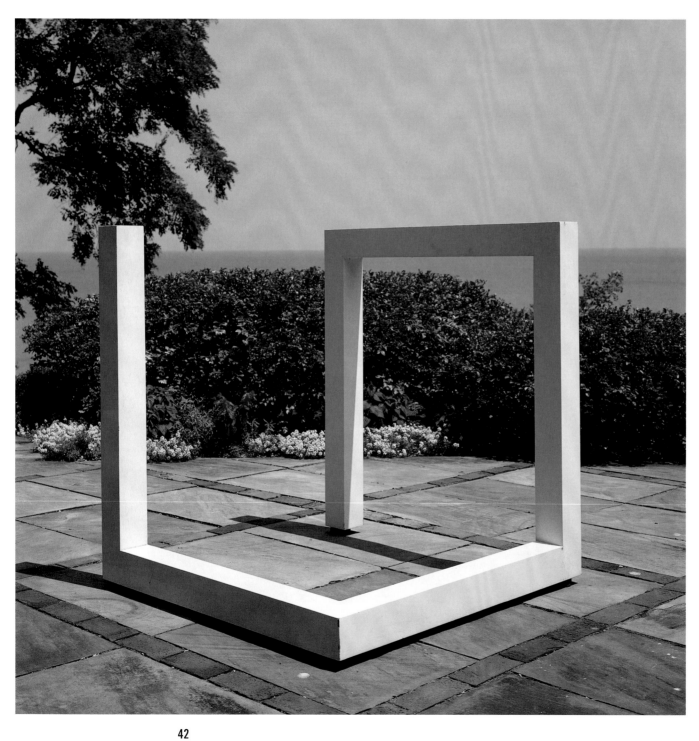

CAT. 44 - VIEW 1
INCOMPLETE OPEN CUBE 6/13, 1974
PAINTED ALUMINUM
40 X 40 X 40"
KARLA AND WALTER M. GOLDSCHMIDT

42

CAT. 44 - VIEW 2
INCOMPLETE OPEN CUBE 6/13, 1974
PAINTED ALUMINUM
40 X 40 X 40"
KARLA AND WALTER M. GOLDSCHMIDT

CAT. 48
INCOMPLETE OPEN CUBE 6/24, 1974
PAINTED ALUMINUM
40 X 40 X 40"
HERBERT LUST GALLERY

SCHEMATIC DRAWING FOR
INCOMPLETE OPEN CUBE 6/24, 1974
INK AND PENCIL ON VELLUM
12 X 12"
THE LEWITT COLLECTION,
CHESTER, CONNECTICUT
(NOT INCLUDED IN EXHIBITION)

6/24 X

CAT. 48
INCOMPLETE OPEN CUBE 6/24, 1974
PAINTED ALUMINUM
40 X 40 X 40"
HERBERT LUST GALLERY

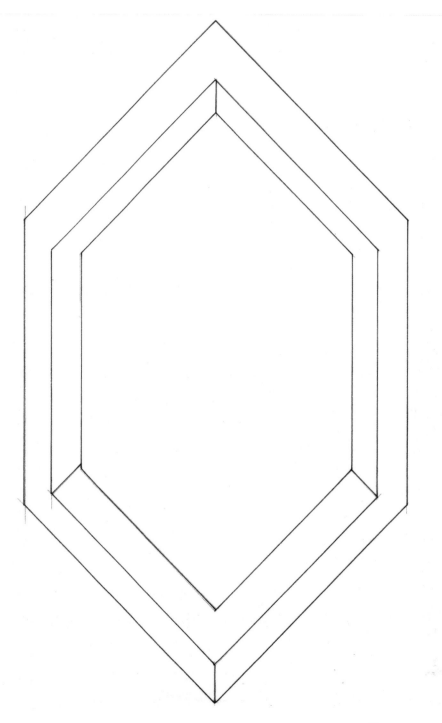

CAT. 33
6/24 FROM
SCHEMATIC DRAWINGS FOR
INCOMPLETE OPEN CUBES, 1974
INK AND PENCIL ON VELLUM
131 PARTS
12 X 12" EACH
THE LEWITT COLLECTION,
CHESTER, CONNECTICUT

6/24

LeWitt

CAT. 33
SIX PART VARIATIONS FROM
SCHEMATIC DRAWINGS FOR
INCOMPLETE OPEN CUBES, 1974
INK AND PENCIL ON VELLUM
131 PARTS
12 X 12" EACH
THE LEWITT COLLECTION,
CHESTER, CONNECTICUT

PHASE PIECE

PAMELA M. LEE

THOSE WHO UNDERSTAND ART ONLY BY WHAT IT LOOKS LIKE OFHOSE WHO UNDERSTAND VERY MUCH AT ALL. SOL LEWITT[1]

THOSE WHO UNDERSTAND ART ONLY BY WHAT IT LOOKS LIKE OFTEN DO NOT UNDERSTAND VERY MUCH AT ALL. SOL LEWITT[1]

HEARING SOL LEWITT

In April 1973, a year before he was to exhibit the *Variations of Incomplete Open Cubes,* Sol LeWitt sent the editors of *Flash Art* a letter in which the above citation appears. He was responding to an advertisement placed in the magazine two issues earlier, a bluntly worded attack accusing him of copying several European artists and then claiming their "innovation" as his own. LeWitt's riposte, by contrast, is a model of subtlety and even-handedness. At once pointed and instructive, it sounds a cautionary note against drawing neat equivalences between works of art that are only superficially alike. Such an erroneous approach to the business of interpretation, known to art historians as "pseudo-morphology," is content to view visually comparable works as one and the same thing. It takes objects at face value and fetishizes appearance without regard to history, idea, process. Against such tendencies, which vulgarize the formalist impulses of postwar criticism, LeWitt offered a stern reproach: "Those who understand art only by what it looks like," he wrote, "often do not understand very much at all."

1.
Sol LeWitt, "Comments on an Advertisement Published in *Flash Art*," in *Sol LeWitt: Critical Texts* (hereafter *SLCT*), ed.Adachiara Zevi, (Rome: I Libri di AEIOU, 1994), p. 99.

2.
For one (unintentionally) parodic response to such a question, see the video by John Baldessari, *Baldessari Sings LeWitt,* in which Baldessari recorded himself woozily crooning the "Sentences on Conceptual Art" to the tune of the "Star Spangled Banner," among other popular numbers.

3.
For an introduction to this problem, see Edward Strickland, *Minimalism* (Bloomington Hills: Indiana University Press, 1993).

This statement is consistent with LeWitt's longstanding beliefs. In his "Paragraphs on Conceptual Art" (1967), and "Sentences on Conceptual Art" (1969), two of the most important art critical texts of the 1960s, LeWitt challenges the preeminence of the formal and the visual within the history of art and crystallizes a radically divergent move in postwar practice towards the conceptual and idea-based. For the purposes of this essay, however, his words serve another, certainly linked, rhetorical possibility. What if we were to push LeWitt's proposition to its logical extreme? In pondering his statement, I wondered if his words could apply to *other* senses beyond the visual altogether. What, for instance, would his works *sound* like, the *Variations of Incomplete Open Cubes* in particular?

Admittedly, this is an absurd question and may appear to generate equally unlikely responses.[2] But the answer I propose in my discussion of the *Variations of Incomplete Open Cubes* is neither so literal nor so metaphorical as these questions seem to imply. My claim is that certain principles of contemporary music can serve as models in interpreting LeWitt's work, illuminating aspects of his "structures" (as he prefers to call his three dimensional objects) that are otherwise suppressed when treated through visual terms exclusively. I will focus on the musical process of "phasing" or "phase-shifting" associated with the mid-sixties through early seventies work of the so-called "minimalist" composer Steve Reich and his seminal experiments in taped music. Briefly put, phasing is a compositional process in which two or more identical audio loops are played simultaneously, repeated extensively as an uninterrupted duration, and then allowed to slip — at first, gradually and then, with gathering velocity — out of synch with one another. Though the results of this process might seem reductive at best, crushingly monotonous at worst, the music that emerges in the gap between the loops is both startling and unexpectedly resonant. That resonance carries with it significant structural implications for the *Incomplete Open Cubes.*

From the mid-sixties through the early seventies, several music critics identified the relationship between LeWitt and his contemporary musical peers, treating their affinities primarily as a function of social influence.[3] My account, by contrast, is not directed to questions of influence as much as it is heuristic, seeing phasing as parallel to LeWitt's

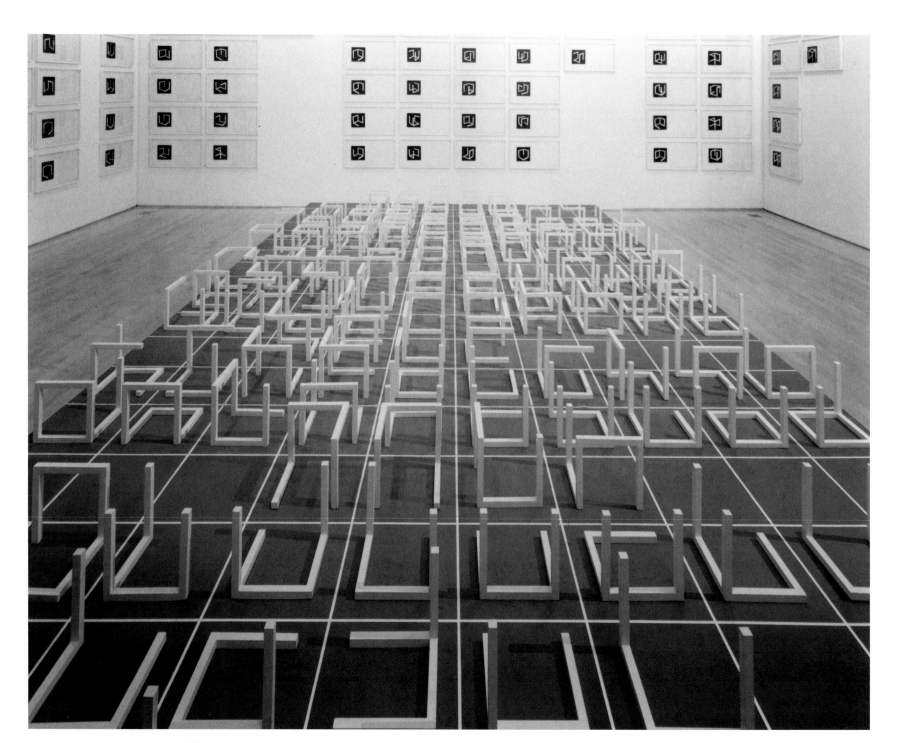

working process. Properties of phasing not only speak to issues of interpretation in the *Variations of Incomplete Open Cubes*, I want to argue, but also shed light on larger phenomena undergirding the art of the period, a period I claim approaches the perceptual condition known as synethesia.

VARIATIONS IN CONTEXT:

SERIALISM, MINIMALISM AND CONCEPTUAL ART WITH A SMALL "C."

We first need to consider the production and reception of the *Variations of Incomplete Open Cubes*, the pivotal role they occupy within the artist's oeuvre, and the problems of categorization that have long attended the criticism of his work. As a multi-part, multi-media piece (hence the "variations" of the title), the *Variations of Incomplete Open Cubes* consists of isometric drawings, photographs, a book, singular structures and most centrally, a large series of 122 skeletal wooden units, each measuring 8 inches on its side, and each sequentially laid out on a grey, gridded field (figure 1). The open cubes themselves were generated from a paradoxically simple plan: a *complete* investigation into how one might *not* complete the form of a cube. Beginning with a modular unit of three edges (the minimum number of sides that can imply the three-dimensionality of a cube), and ending with one structure with eleven edges (the last functioning variant of an incomplete cube), LeWitt multiplied the configuration of each structure as determined by the number of sides from three to eleven.

While the idea driving the work was straightforward enough, the solution seemingly neat and economical, the production was anything but. "It was hideous," LeWitt recalled of the maddening process of envisioning and distributing the forms in space; "...Because I didn't want to repeat the same image in a different position, each image was in itself, unique..."

> SO DOING LITTLE DRAWINGS WAS ONE PROCESS AND MAKING LITTLE MODELS OUT OF PAPER CLIPS WAS ANOTHER. I WOULD MAKE A DRAWING OF ONE OF THE CUBES. THEN I'D MAKE A LITTLE MODEL WITH A PAPERCLIP AND TURN IT AROUND TO MAKE SURE THAT I DIDN'T REPEAT IN OTHER WAYS. AND I FOUND, SOME-TIMES, THAT I HAD REPEATED THE POSITION.[4]

This is a portrait of the artist as frustrated being. To be sure, the image of LeWitt's bending and twisting his paperclips into so many working models was only compounded by the virtual expansion of the project into mixed media.

4.
Sol LeWitt, "A Conversation with Gary Garrels," interview by Gary Garrels, in *Open: Magazine of the San Francisco Museum of Modern Art*, no.1, (Winter/Spring 2000): p. 31.
5.
Sol LeWitt, "Serial Project No. 1 (ABCD)," in *SLCT*, p. 75.

Few of LeWitt's works have generated so much critical controversy as the *Incomplete Open Cubes*, not that it was produced *ex nihilio*. Its ground had been prepared some eight years earlier by the artist's larger investigation into serial structures and systems-based procedures. In 1966, LeWitt describes this practice in a statement on his *Serial Project #1 (ABCD)*, (figure 2). "Serial compositions," he wrote,

> ARE MULTIPART PIECES WITH REGULATED CHANGES. THE DIFFERENCES BETWEEN THE PARTS ARE THE SUBJECT OF THE COMPOSITION. IF SOME PARTS REMAIN CON-STANT, IT IS TO PUNCTUATE THE CHANGES.... THE SERIES WOULD BE READ BY THE VIEWER IN A LINEAR OR NARRATIVE MANNER EVEN THOUGH IN ITS FINAL FORM MANY OF THESE SETS WOULD BE OPERATING SIMULTANEOUSLY, MAKING COMPRE-HENSION DIFFICULT. THE AIM OF THE ARTIST WOULD NOT BE TO INSTRUCT THE VIEWER BUT TO GIVE HIM INFORMATION.[5]

FIG. 1

Sol LeWitt
Incomplete Open Cubes, 1974
Installation view, San Francisco Museum of Art
122 painted wood structures on a painted
wooden base and 122 framed photographs
and drawings on paper
Each structure: 8 x 8 x 8"
Base: 12 x 120 x 216"
Each framed element: 14 x 26"
Collection of San Francisco Museum
of Modern Art, Accessions Committee Fund

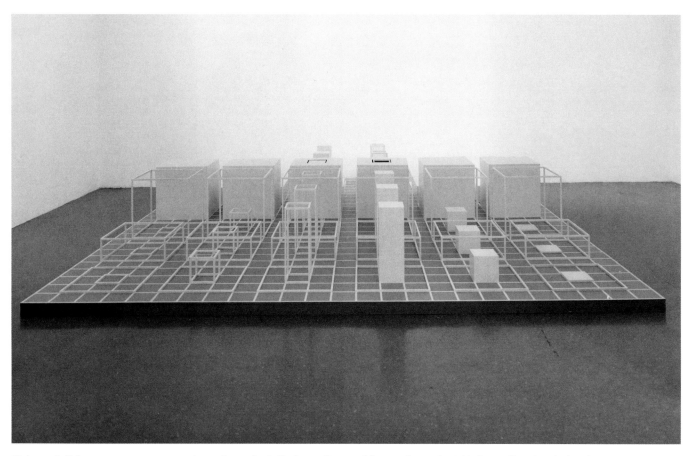

FIG.2

Sol LeWitt,
Serial Project #1 (ABCD), 1966
Baked enamel on aluminum
Collection of The Museum of
Modern Art, New York
Gift of Agnes Gund and purchase
(by exchange)

It is a striking passage, as much as for what it *doesn't* consider as for what it does. Emphasis is given to process, organization, reception, far less to the "look" of the object in question.

Serial processes may have been crucial to the artist, but little comprehension of this is evident among the contemporary criticism surrounding his work. No doubt, with its modular forms, stern geometry and substantial dependence on the grid, LeWitt's art of the period *seems* to square with the popular (or superficial) critical understanding of minimalist sculpture in the mid-sixties, which saw his art as so many dumb solids. "Seems" is the operative word here, for LeWitt and many of his peers were quick to dismiss the minimalist label altogether. The artist humorously observed of this tag in his "Paragraphs on Conceptual Art":

RECENTLY THERE HAS BEEN MUCH WRITTEN ABOUT MINIMAL ART, BUT I HAVE NOT DISCOVERED ANYONE WHO ADMITS TO DOING THIS KIND OF THING. THERE ARE OTHER ART FORMS AROUND CALLED PRIMARY STRUCTURES, REDUCTIVE, REJECTIVE, COOL AND MINI-ART. NO ARTIST I KNOW WILL OWN UP TO ANY OF THESE EITHER. THEREFORE I CONCLUDE THAT IT IS PART OF A SECRET LANGUAGE THAT ART CRITICS USE WHEN COMMUNICATING WITH EACH OTHER THROUGH THE MEDIUM OF THE ART MAGAZINE. MINI-ART IS BEST BECAUSE IT REMINDS ONE OF MINISKIRTS AND LONG-LEGGED GIRLS. IT MUST REFER TO VERY SMALL WORKS OF ART.[6]

6.
Sol LeWitt, "Paragraphs on Conceptual Art," in *SLCT*, p.80.

The paragraph reads as (and no doubt is) a winking rejoinder to both the jargon and hype of the contemporary art magazine, but it also attests to the confusion critics faced in bracketing much art of the time. Consider, for instance, how this statement on minimalism arrives in the format of LeWitt's "Paragraphs on Conceptual Art," his droll, rather than dogmatic, tract that famously announces "what the work of art looks like isn't too important." Written one year after LeWitt's "Serial Projects," the "Paragraphs" lay further stress on the alliance between process and idea in his work, neatly overturning the cliche of his art as reductive and blank. And just as he playfully derides the category of minimalism, LeWitt also suggests a tacit resistance to art critical categories in general. If LeWitt's work was henceforth deemed conceptual, it was, as he once described it, conceptual "with a small c."[7]

To the extent that LeWitt questioned these art critical determinations, so too were writers polarized as to the perceptual effect his modular forms produced. When the *Variations of Incomplete Open Cubes* was first shown in 1974 at the Galerie Yvon Lambert in Paris and the John Weber Gallery in New York, a number of important critics (Rosalind Krauss, Donald Kuspit, Lucy Lippard, Joseph Masheck) weighed in on the topic. The dominant camp regarded the *Incomplete Open Cubes* as an exercise in rationality, as though "LeWitt's modular consistencency illustrates the idea of art as a realm of essential order."[8] Here, then, was the vision of LeWitt as a Conceptualist with a big "C." Donald Kuspit argued in calling Sol LeWitt's work "the look of thought" that: "LeWitt's objects barely generate any sensuous intensity, and instead seem to demand an intellectual response.

... IN OTHER WORDS, IN LOOKING AT LEWITT'S OBJECTS, ONE DOES NOT SO MUCH SEE THEM AS THINK ABOUT THEM.[9]

One does not so much see them as think about them. In claiming that LeWitt's was an art of almost mathematical intellection, perhaps Kuspit took the artist's statements on conceptual art a little too literally. Certainly LeWitt's texts represented a decided move away from the visual in the judging of art, but they did not treat the "non-visual" or "non-sensuous" as the raison d'etre of his work.[10]

7. On his satirizing "the more advanced conceptualists," see, e.g., "Sol LeWitt Interviewed," interview by Andrew Wilson, in *SLCT*, p. 125.

8. Donald Kuspit, "Sol LeWitt: The Look of Thought," in *SLCT*, p. 211.

9. Kuspit, p. 210.

10. Artists quickly seized on the absurdity of producing a wholly "non-visual" work of art. See, e.g., Mel Bochner, "Excerpts from Speculation (1967-1970)," *Artforum 8*, no. 9 (May 1970): p. 70; and Daniel Buren, "Mise en Gard," in *Konzeption/Conception* (Leverkusen, Germany: Stüdtischen Museum, 1969).

11. Rosalind Krauss, "LeWitt in Progress," in *SLCT*, p. 22.

In stark contrast to Kuspit, Rosalind Krauss sees little if nothing mathematical in LeWitt's *Incomplete Open Cubes*, and she is equally impatient with the argument that this is work borne of rational motivations. For her, LeWitt is neither a mathematician *nor* a humanist, but a figure of radical incongruity — one who once claimed that "conceptual artists are mystics and not rationalists" and whose generation was swayed less by Euclid then the absurdist poetics of a Samuel Beckett or an Alain Robbe-Grillet. In her essay "LeWitt in Progress," Krauss argues that the "look of thought" to which LeWitt's work may appear to subscribe masks an almost compulsive, and therefore irrational, exploration of serial procedures. It was an exploration that exposes reason as necessarily limned by the obsessive, a point she expresses cogently when she writes, "The babble of a LeWitt serial expansion has nothing of the economy of a mathematician's language. It has the loquaciousness of the speech of children or the very old, in that its refusal to summarize, to use the single example that would imply the whole, is like those feverish accounts of events composed of a string of almost identical details, connected by 'and.'"[11]

Krauss uses catachresis not merely for literary effect, but also to appeal to the *embodiedness* of LeWitt's art, its phenomenological density. But this sense of embodiedness, positioned as it is against the transcendental ideal of Kuspit's account, is also conveyed through her invocation of sound in LeWitt's art: the "on and on" quality of the cubes as they seem to echo and ping throughout space as a kind of visual glossolalia. It is at this point that we come full circle to the peculiar musicality of LeWitt's *Variations* and its more specific correspondance with the principle of phasing.

RESONANCES:

LEWITT, CONTEMPORARY MUSIC AND THE SYNESTHETIC CONDITION

LeWitt's great love for and engagement with music is well-established. Relations between the artist and musicians such as Reich and Philip Glass are consistent throughout his career. In one of the most fascinating of LeWitt's photographic books, his *Autobiography* of 1980, for example, LeWitt devotes a gridded spread to his extensive record and tape collection, among which albums by both composers prominently occupy two squares (figure 3). A survey of the holdings of LeWitt's collection at the Wadsworth Atheneum confirms this engagement in another dimension. Alongside works by friends and peers such as Eva Hesse and Robert Smithson, Hannah Darboven and Adrian Piper, are scores by Reich and Glass, sometimes purchased by the artist to support his friends during leaner times (figure 4).

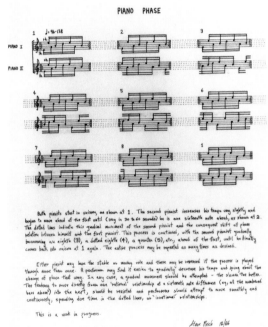

FIG.3

Sol LeWitt,
Autobiography (detail), 1980
Black and white photographs
mounted on paper
62 sheets, each: 12 x 22"
The LeWitt Collection,
Chester, Connecticut

FIG.4

Steve Reich,
Phase Piece, 1966
Ink on paper
13 1/4 x 11"
The LeWitt Collection,
courtesy of the Wadsworth
Atheneum Museum of Art,
Hartford

Where is one to locate these observations in relationship to LeWitt's oeuvre? Because the more than passing exchange between LeWitt and several musicians points well beyond seemingly incidental social phenomena, it would be wise to look at the *Variations* as more than a mere reflection of the artist's personal tastes. It attests to the porosity between the social worlds of the plastic arts and contemporary music in New York in the sixties and early seventies and undermines our presumptions about the separateness of the two fields. Today one might think, however mistakenly, of these worlds as mutually exclusive. (A concert by the Kronos Quartet, for instance, might be envisioned at a geographical remove from the art world bustle of a Chelsea or a SoHo.) Yet in the sixties, when many contemporary composers were struggling to find an audience, it was not the rarefied habitus of classical music that embraced them, but the equally struggling sites of a burgeoning New York art world and its alternative performance and exhibition spaces. Examples are numerous: Yoko Ono's downtown loft and its series of concerts staged by LaMonte Young in the early sixties; countless intermedia performances at the Judson Memorial Church; SoHo's 115 Greene Street and other ramshackle operations in the seventies. The proliferation of these spaces signals a virtual mixing of artistic media, turning away from high modernist conceptions of the arts as materially self-sufficient and genre-bound.[12]

Reich's particular position in this history is instructive. By necessity, he often performed in venues associated with the art world business of minimalism (e.g. the Park Place Gallery), so that many of his earliest followers in New York were artists. By 1969, Reich was invited to participate in an important exhibition at the Whitney Museum of American Art entitled "Anti-Illusion: Procedures/Materials." Devoted to questions of process — the relationship between art and the procedural conditions of its own making — the show included the time-based media of film and music in addition to work by Hesse, Bruce Nauman, Richard Serra, Carl Andre, Lynda Benglis and other visual artists.

12. In 1979, LeWitt produced a black and white film for the performance "Dance" as part of a collaboration with Lucinda Childs and Philip Glass at the Brooklyn Academy of Music.
13. Steve Reich, "Music as a Gradual Process," reprinted in *Steve Reich: Writings about Music,* (Halifax: The Press of the Nova Scotia College of Art and Design, 1974), pp. 9-10.
14. See, e.g., Reich's statements to the contrary in Steve Reich, "An Interview with Composer Steve Reich," interview by Emily Wasserman, *Artforum 10*, no.9, (May 1972): pp. 44-48; Steve Reich, "Steve Reich," interview by Michael Nyman," *Studio International*, 192, (November 1976): pp. 300-307.

It was on the occasion of the Whitney exhibition that Reich performed his "Pendulum Music" with the assistance of James Tenny, Snow, Nauman and Serra, and produced a short text which seemed to provide a theoretical foundation for what was otherwise a social relation between the various groups participating. In "Music as a Gradual Process," Reich wrote, "The distinctive thing about musical processes is that they determine all the note-to-note (sound-to-sound) details and the over all form simultaneously. (Think of a round or infinite canon.)

I AM INTERESTED IN PERCEPTIBLE PROCESSES. I WANT TO BE ABLE TO HEAR THE PROCESS HAPPENING THROUGHOUT THE SOUNDING MUSIC....THOUGH I MAY HAVE THE PLEASURE OF DISCOVERING MUSICAL PROCESSES AND COMPOSING THE MUSICAL MATERIAL TO RUN THROUGH THEM, ONCE THE PROCESS IS SET UP AND LOADED, IT RUNS BY ITSELF.[13]

It is hard for the art historian not to hear LeWitt's own thinking reverberate throughout this passage. Indeed, some critics seized upon the the notion that Reich's conception of "music as process" followed contemporary art, an idea which was just as swiftly rejected by the artist.[14] English composer and erstwhile critic Michael Nyman, most prominent among the writers, saw in Reich's fascination with process an analogue to Sol LeWitt's statements on conceptual art. In 1968 — a year before the Whitney show — Nyman had already applied the term "minimalism" to this new music, self-consciously appropriating the rhetoric of the visual arts in the process. For critics such as Nyman, this new body of work — also referred to as pulse music, electric music and even "needle-stuck-in-the-groove" music — mirrored the structural forms of its earlier plastic counterparts. It was a music of reduced, repetitive forms, bereft of narratival or figurative development and — to follow its most vociferous detractors — deadly boring, without emotional affect, and produced with neither skill nor technique. The mirroring was reciprocal in another sense, as the musicians lumped under the minimalist banner (Terry Riley, LaMonte Young, Glass, Reich, a few European figures) rejected the term just as visual artists had several years previously. They were just as quick to challenge the impact of the plastic arts on their music as superficial; and, in an understandable bid for compositional autonomy, attempted to distance their work from their musical peers.

It is important to note that the "trickle down" theory of minimalist art's influence on music was unidirectional: few have bothered to reverse the analogy from music *to* art. To do so, however, is a matter of both historical and methodological importance. Considering properties of music traditionally excluded from discussions of object-based art highlights a paradigm shift taking place in the plastic arts in the sixties and seventies. Beyond this, it challenges the attribution of chronological influence from one practice to the next, wreaking havoc with models of historical influence as so many dots on a plane, waiting to be connected. This is where the principle of phasing becomes especially useful.

We've already noted that phasing or "phase-shifting" grew out of Reich's taped work in the mid-sixties. In his seminal pieces "It's Gonna Rain" (1965) and "Come Out" (1966), Reich recorded a singular passage, repeated the loop on two or more recorders at the same time, and let the passages fall progressively *out* of synch with one another, exploiting an initial technological defect in the machines for striking compositional ends. Audio loops were "found," everyday and vernacular, but nonetheless were selected for their particular and at times, symbolic resonance. ("It's Gonna Rain," for instance, was recorded in San Franciso's Union Square during a sermon of gravely apocalyptic undertones delivered by one Brother Walker.) Hence the audio passage acted as the driving idea for Reich's work, and the permutation of the idea, expressed as a musical duration, provides the armature for the entire piece. By the late sixties, when Reich began to consider the taping process exhausted, he extended the device of phasing through less technological means. In pieces such as "Piano Phase" (1967) he started to apply its principles to the performance of live music, so that two or more musicians might produce its effects in concert, a feat requiring profound concentration and almost atheletic displays of endurance.

Phasing finds precedent in pre-modern musical composition. To repeat Reich's words in "Music as a Gradual Process:" "Think of a round or infinite canon." Like a round, phasing dramatizes the peculiar relationship between part and whole in the perception of music. Phasing draws upon the persistence of a singular passage which can be quickly grasped, and its subsequent disconnection between the totality of the piece is experienced as indivisible in time. Unlike the rounds of one's childhood, however, so simple as to be understood almost immediately, phasing produces the paradoxical condition of *non-comprehension,* in spite of its structural (even mathematical) legibility. The process itself might be perceptible, but the results aren't necessarily so. As musical loops or words are repeated seemingly ad infinitum, the consequence is not so much reduction or perceptual clarity (however stripped down the process, there is nothing minimal about it), but expansion, a shuddering of sound felt like an echo. What is produced in the slippage of two identical passages is all at once shimmering, austere and cacaphonous, the effect only increased by increments as the work is apprehended in time.

Far more than reading the *Incomplete Open Cubes* as mathematical, abstract and reasoned, phasing as a model for the plastic arts reveals the importance of duration, aggregation and incompletion. Phasing stresses how duration is internalized within both the work's making and perception; and duration, in its turn, forges the missing link between fragment and totality, module and unity in understanding LeWitt's structure. Understanding LeWitt's work, in other words, bears strong parallels to analyzing the temporal principles inherent in phasing. Think, for instance, of how the mind attempts to grasp one module of the cube at a time, just as one attempts to isolate a musical passage from the larger context of a phase piece. Think too, how we struggle to intuit the difference between one multi-sided cube from its adjacent counterpart, just as we struggle to intuit the gradual shift between one incomplete cube and its subsequent increment. No wonder that LeWitt described the labor of working out his forms in space as "hideous." It is the interpretive labor of continuously shifting between the beginning of one passage and the next; or of attempting to render such distinctions meaningful in the first place; or of shuttling between forms that teeter on the brink of indistinguishability. For the knowledge of a single element in the *Incomplete Open Cubes* is meaningful *only* in relationship to the larger system understood as a unity in time; and that unity is itself a slippery and precarious thing. Like an early phase piece by Reich, which extends a legible musical passage to the point of its aural illegibility, LeWitt's work doggedly moves toward its own *perceptual* incompletion.

We should pause to take measure of another intepretation, to leaven what might otherwise seem an exercise in intellectual frustration. As Rosalind Krauss importantly warns, the *Incomplete Open Cubes* cannot be reduced to the status of a theoretical proof or brain-teaser; and indeed, treating the work through the terms of phasing supports her model. The perceptual sparring that takes place between part and whole in the group actually *harmonizes* for its audience an

15.

LeWitt, "Comments on an Advertisement Published in *Flash Art*," p. 98.

almost sensuous vibration between idea and form: the inseparability of LeWitt's system from its concrete presentation. One of the most enduring conventions of music holds that musical concept is utterly indissociable from musical form – the notion that one can't separate the "idea" of the music from its expression in performance. The *Incomplete Open Cubes* emphasizes this conceit in the plastic arts. "My own work of the past ten years is about only one thing," LeWitt wrote in 1973, "logical statements using formal elements as grammar."[15] By using logical statements explicitly as a formal element, the artist points to the intractability of content or idea (his statements) and the means by which they are communicated.

The temporal principles of phasing specifically, and music more generally, are also at play in the drawings, photographs, single modules and book that accompany the structural installation, the *Variations of Incomplete Open Cubes*. These principles revolve around the concept of variation, and the ways in which these terms translate into the respective domains of music and art. To call a musical composition a "variation," after all, invokes the exploration of its structure as it is fragmented, expanded, compressed, sped up, slowed down and augmented throughout its performance. It unearths the multiple and surprising colorations that derive from the most rudimentary musical structure. Musical variation and repetition converge seamlessly in this regard: aural difference emerges within the space of repetition. But while the variation is standard to the performance and composition of music, it does not rest as easily with the traditions of art history. Artists have *always* returned to and repeated the same theme or motif within their work, but the idea that such practices represent the end-goal of art-making itself is a matter of far more recent vintage. Simply stated, such practices undermine the belief in the singularity of the precious and original art object, the hoary, romantic ideal that works of art are born of flashes of almost spiritual inspiration. LeWitt's introduction of the term "variation" into the realm of the plastic arts necessarily challenges this critical tradition as it acknowledges, whether purposefully or inadvertently, a compositional strategy commonplace to music.

Phasing itself theatricalizes the rules of variation in at least two important ways. In its insistence on repetition – in its endeavor to squeeze every sonic possibility out of a singular musical passage – it aligns itself fundamentally with processes of variation. Secondly and more specifically, phasing compounds this effect by running identical passages against one another, compressing the principles of a musical variation into a unified whole. As if exploring and mapping this idea in plastic form, LeWitt's multiple presentations of the *Incomplete Open Cubes* speak to the coexistence of manifold variations of the same theme, and reinforce the necessarily "incomplete" dimension of the piece in the process. Here photography mingles with drawings, which mingle with structures which are then presented as a book: each acts as supplements to one another while retaining its separate identity as an object. The grouping of these works, then, is something of an ersatz totality, one that recognizes the *failure* to be totalized along genre determinations alone, as it always — like the cubes themselves — remains open. In this regard, the *Variations* demonstrates a marked kinship with LeWitt's other projects. His well-known *Wall Drawings*, for instance, offer the possibilty of being executed in different locales by different hands, so that the driving concept of the work functions as a musical score does, enabling a wealth of new variations with each iteration in time.

The application of phasing to the realm of the visual arts ultimately brings with it a challenge of both interpretative and historical consequences. For what does it mean to evoke one sense faculty — the capacity to hear — in the material domain of another — the visual field? What, if any, historical implications arise from this linkage? The idea that one might "touch light," "smell shape" or "hear a LeWitt" for that matter, belongs to a longer scientific and literary tradition centered around a condition known as synesthesia, a peculiar intermingling of the senses. Synesthesia occurs when a stimulus received by one sense triggers its sensual response in another sense modality. It is as if synapses had been crosswired or confused, perceptual networks entangled with one another. Synesthesia may be involuntary (and therefore, a perceptual and/or physiological condition) or find metaphorical expression in literature, music and the plastic arts. In the latter case, it speaks to a deepening integration of the senses, reflecting a deepening of aesthetic appreciation as well.[16]

Modernists ranging from Kandinsky to Delauney to Scriabin to Messiaen have long made use of synesthetic metaphors in writing on their respective practices. Yet the synesthestic dimension of the *Variations of Incomplete Open Cubes* prompts an analysis of decidedly contemporary import, a condition peculiar to LeWitt's generation of artists. Less at stake here is the symbolist appeal to the human sensorium than is a virtual erasure of the apartheid between the senses: that is, their organization as autonomous and experienced in isolation, and the division of the arts respectively assigned to each. In this regard, not only do the *Variations* offer a retreat from the weight placed on the visual within high modernism, but they also suggest both a border crossing and an opening in the apprehension of the arts in the postwar period. This crossing, we could say, underscores the transgression of genres that emerged with LeWitt's community of artists in the sixties and the seventies, and the perceptual and interpretive skills each require. It signals, by extension, a proliferation of new media's strategies beyond the categories of painting and sculpture (video, performance, site works and installation, a use of photography beyond its documentary impulses, etc.); the refusal of artists to be limited by formalism's imperatives alone; and artists' treatment of art as a system, linked serially to other communicative systems, whether musical, cinematic, linguistic or pop cultural. This crossing is played out in LeWitt's *Variations,* and is dramatized when his process is considered through phasing's terms. In analogizing musical variation as the mutability of art itself, his is a practice which remains happily open and necessarily incomplete.

16.
The literature on synethesia is wide-ranging, and may be divided into artistic and scientific approaches. For a very useful introduction to the theme, see Greta Berman, "Synethesia and the Arts," *Leonardo*, 32, no.1., (1999): pp. 15-22. The entire issue is devoted to the concept.

1. AB BC CD DA AE BF CG x①.

2. AB BC CD DA AE BF EF  x③.

3. AB BC CD DA AE BF FG x⑥.

4. AB BC CD DA AE BF HE 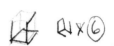 x⑦.

5. AB BC CD DA AE CG EF 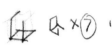 x④.

6. AB BC CD DA AE CG FG  x⑤.

7. AB BC CD DA AE EF FG  ㉒.

8. AB BC CD DA AE EF HE  x⑳.

9. AB BC CD DA BF EF HE  x㉑.

10. AB BC CD AE BF CG DH  x②.

11. AB BC CD AE BF CG GH 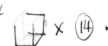 x⑭.

12. AB BC CD AE BF CG HE 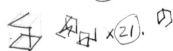 x⑩.

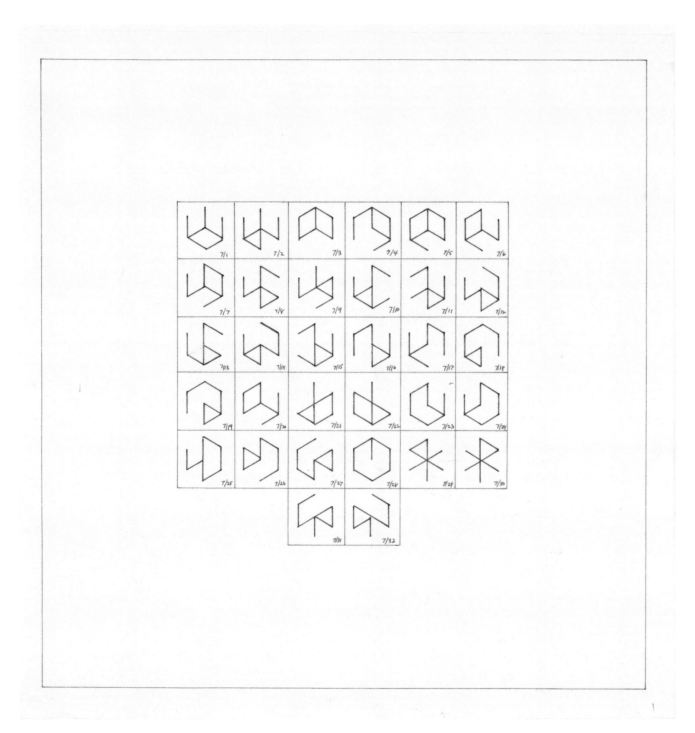

CAT. 33
*SEVEN PART VARIATIONS FROM
SCHEMATIC DRAWINGS FOR
INCOMPLETE OPEN CUBES*, 1974
INK AND PENCIL ON VELLUM
131 PARTS
12 X 12" EACH
THE LEWITT COLLECTION,
CHESTER, CONNECTICUT

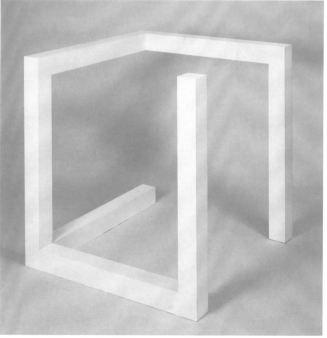

CLOCKWISE FROM TOP
CAT. 49
INCOMPLETE OPEN CUBE 7/5, 1974
PAINTED ALUMINUM
40 X 40 X 40"
PRIVATE COLLECTION

CAT. 54
INCOMPLETE OPEN CUBE 7/18, 1974
PAINTED ALUMINUM
42 X 42 X 42"
BAYLY MUSEUM, UNIVERSITY OF VIRGINIA.
MUSEUM PURCHASE WITH FUNDS FROM THE
NATIONAL ENDOWMENT FOR THE ARTS AND
THE MEMBERSHIP ART ACQUISITION FUND.
1976.3

CAT. 52
INCOMPLETE OPEN CUBE 7/12, 1974
PAINTED ALUMINUM
40 X 40 X 40"
COLLECTION LOCKHART

CAT. 55
INCOMPLETE OPEN CUBE 7/22, 1974
PAINTED ALUMINUM
42 X 42 X 42"
PRIVATE COLLECTION

CAT. 53
INCOMPLETE OPEN CUBE 7/17, 1974
PAINTED ALUMINUM
40 X 40 X 40"
THE LEWITT COLLECTION,
COURTESY OF THE WADSWORTH ATHENEUM
MUSEUM OF ART, HARTFORD

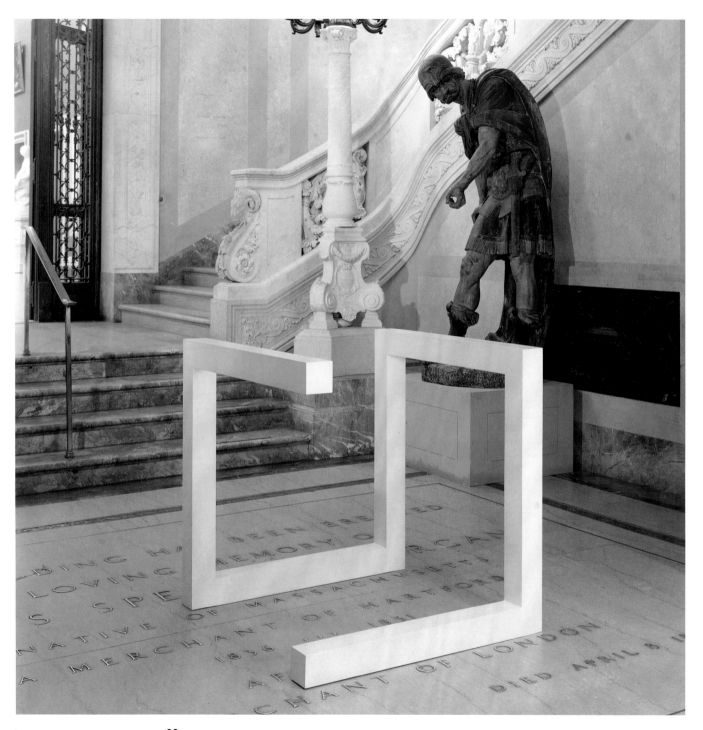

66

CAT. 56
INCOMPLETE OPEN CUBE 7/26, 1974
PAINTED ALUMINUM
40 X 40 X 40"
THE LEWITT COLLECTION,
COURTESY OF THE WADSWORTH
ATHENEUM MUSEUM OF ART,
HARTFORD

PAGES 64-65 AND 72-73
INCOMPLETE OPEN CUBES
INSTALLATION VIEWS
HERBERT LUST GALLERY

CAT. 62
INCOMPLETE OPEN CUBE 8/25, 1974
PAINTED ALUMINUM
40 X 40 X 40"
THE LEWITT COLLECTION,
COURTESY OF THE WADSWORTH
ATHENEUM MUSEUM OF ART,
HARTFORD

PAGES 67-70
INCOMPLETE OPEN CUBES
INSTALLATION VIEWS
WADSWORTH ANTHENEUM
MUSEUM OF ART,
HARTFORD

70

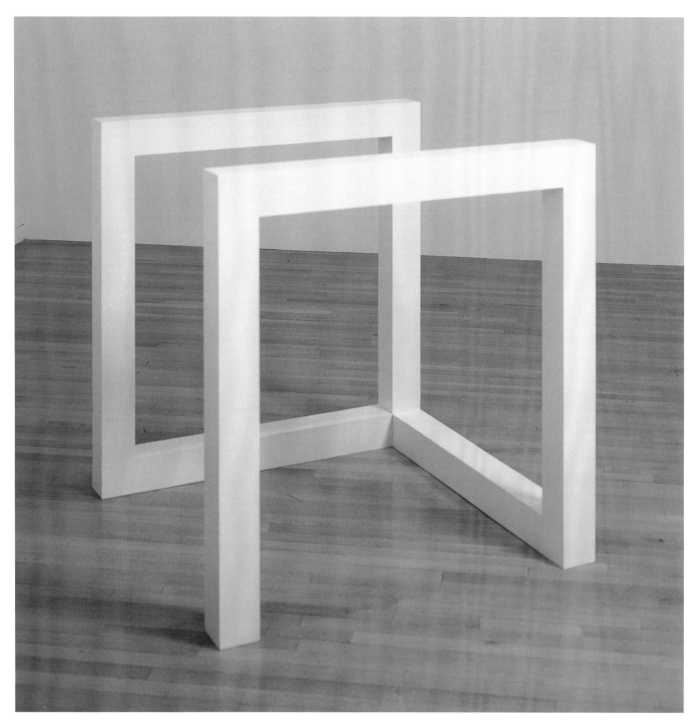

CAT. 61 - VIEW 1
INCOMPLETE OPEN CUBE 8/20, 1974
PAINTED ALUMINUM
42 X 42 X 42"
COLLECTION WEXNER CENTER FOR THE ARTS,
THE OHIO STATE UNIVERSITY;
PURCHASED WITH FUNDS PROVIDED BY
THE NEA IN 1976

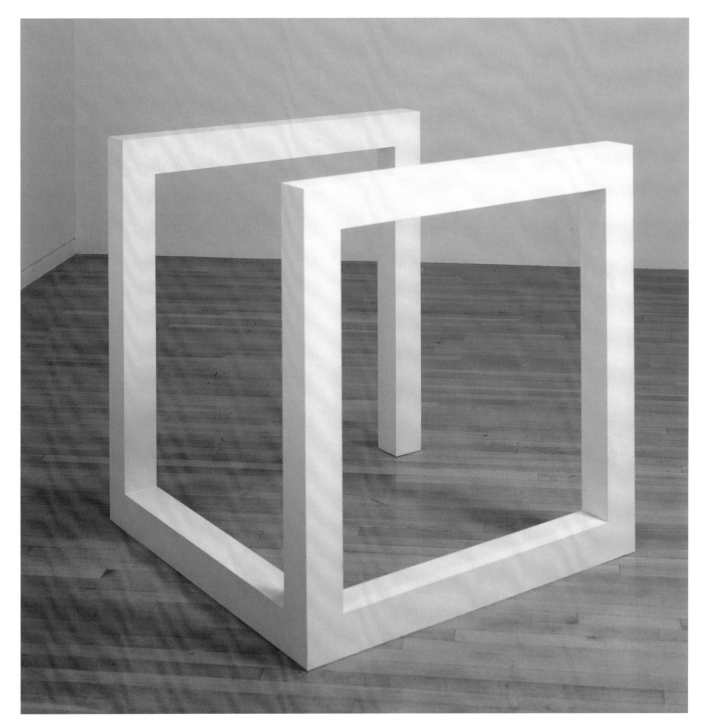

CAT. 61 - VIEW 2
INCOMPLETE OPEN CUBE 8/20, 1974
PAINTED ALUMINUM
42 X 42 X 42"
COLLECTION WEXNER CENTER FOR THE ARTS,
THE OHIO STATE UNIVERSITY;
PURCHASED WITH FUNDS PROVIDED BY
THE NEA IN 1976

8/14

LeWitt

CAT. 33
8/14 FROM
*SCHEMATIC DRAWINGS FOR
INCOMPLETE OPEN CUBES,* 1974
INK AND PENCIL ON VELLUM
131 PARTS
12 X 12" EACH
THE LEWITT COLLECTION,
CHESTER, CONNECTICUT

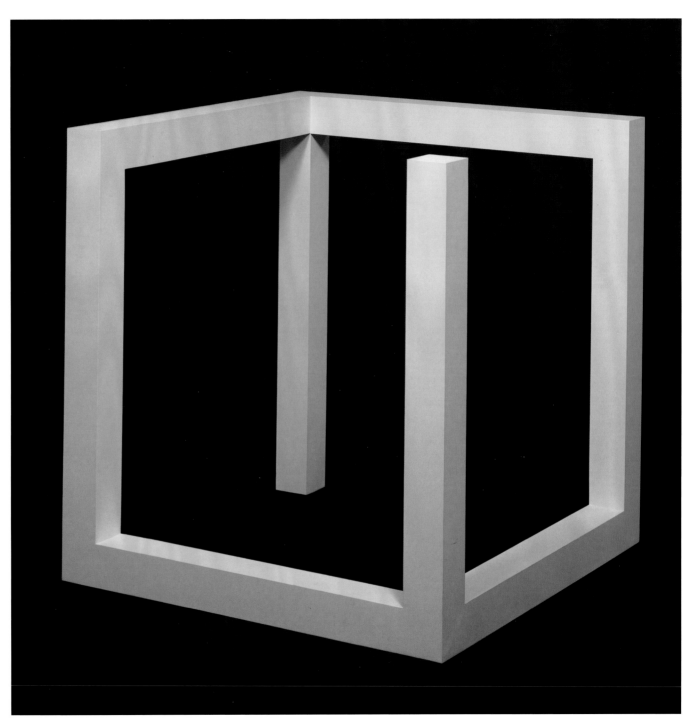

CAT. 60
INCOMPLETE OPEN CUBE 8/14, 1974
PAINTED ALUMINUM
42 X 42 X 42"
HOOD MUSEUM OF ART, DARTMOUTH COLLEGE,
HANOVER, NH;
PURCHASED THROUGH
THE JULIA L. WHITTIER FUND AND
A MATCHING GRANT FROM
THE NATIONAL ENDOWMENT
FOR THE ARTS

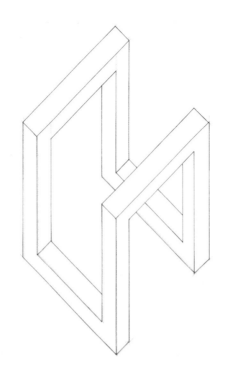

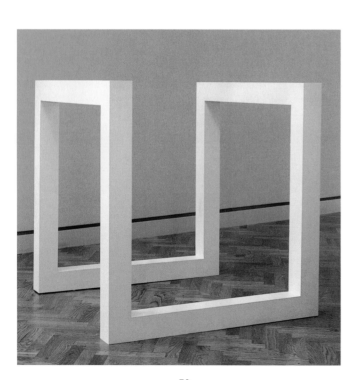

CAT. 33
8/3 FROM
SCHEMATIC DRAWINGS FOR
INCOMPLETE OPEN CUBES, 1974
INK AND PENCIL ON VELLUM
131 PARTS
12 X 12" EACH
THE LEWITT COLLECTION,
CHESTER, CONNECTICUT

CAT. 58 - VIEW 1
INCOMPLETE OPEN CUBE 8/3, 1974
PAINTED ALUMINUM
42 X 42 X 42"
LENT BY THE MINNEAPOLIS INSTITUTE OF ARTS,
GIFT OF MR. AND MRS. MILES O. FITERMAN AND
THE NATIONAL ENDOWMENT
FOR THE ARTS

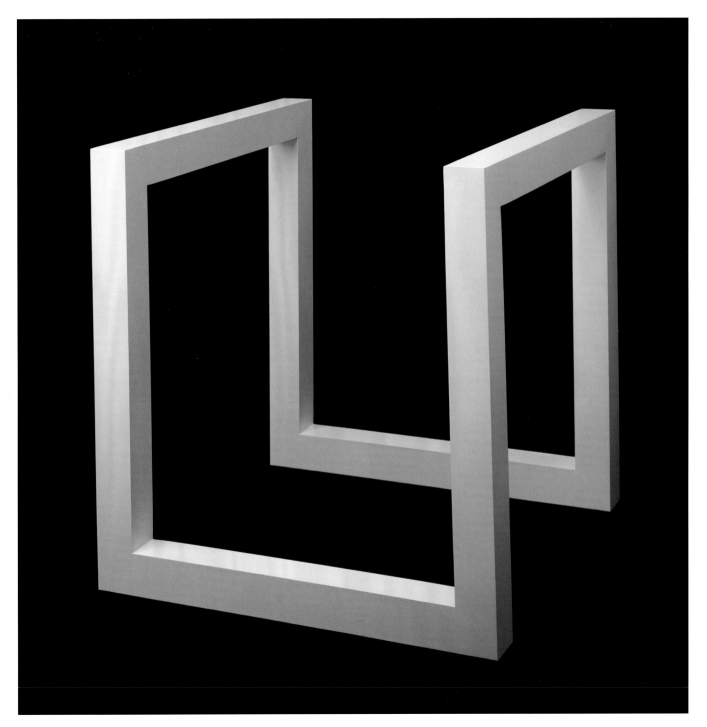

CAT. 58 - VIEW 2
INCOMPLETE OPEN CUBE 8/3, 1974
PAINTED ALUMINUM
42 X 42 X 42"
LENT BY THE MINNEAPOLIS INSTITUTE OF ARTS,
GIFT OF MR. AND MRS. MILES O. FITERMAN
AND THE NATIONAL ENDOWMENT
FOR THE ARTS

CAT. 57
INCOMPLETE OPEN CUBE 8/1, 1974
PAINTED ALUMINUM
40 X 40 X 40"
HERBERT LUST GALLERY

80

CAT. 33
EIGHT PART VARIATIONS FROM
SCHEMATIC DRAWINGS FOR
INCOMPLETE OPEN CUBES, 1974
INK AND PENCIL ON VELLUM
131 PARTS
12 X 12" EACH
THE LEWITT COLLECTION,
CHESTER, CONNECTICUT

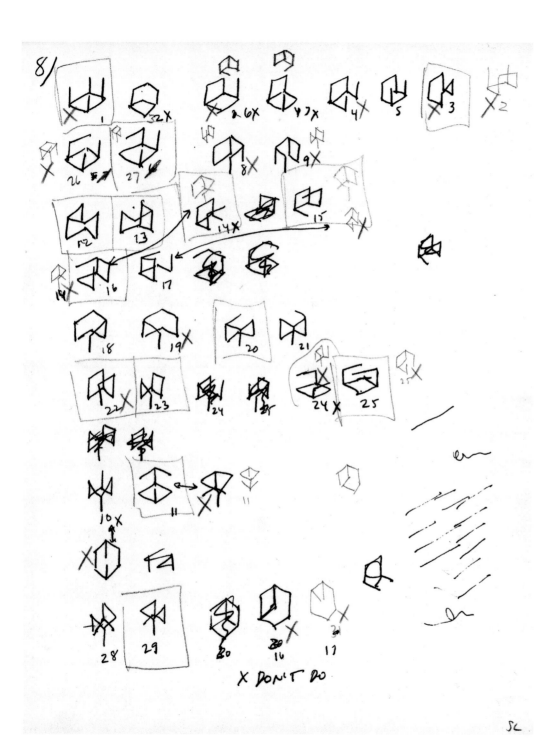

X DON'T DO

CAT. 11
WORKING DRAWING FOR EIGHT-PART
INCOMPLETE OPEN CUBES, 1973-74
INK ON PAPER
11 X 8 1/2"
THE LEWITT COLLECTION,
CHESTER, CONNECTICUT

ART MACHINE

JONATHAN FLATLEY

THE REASON I'M PAINTING THIS WAY IS THAT I WANT TO BE A MACHINE, AND I FEEL WHATEVER I DO AND DO MACHINE-LIKE IS WHAT I WANT TO DO.

— Andy Warhol,
"What is Pop Art?" interview
with G. Swenson, 1963

THE IDEA BECOMES A MACHINE THAT MAKES THE ART.

— Sol LeWitt,
"Paragraphs on Conceptual Art,"
1967

ONE MACHINE IS ALWAYS COUPLED WITH ANOTHER.

— Gilles Deleuze and Felix Guattari,
Anti-Oedipus, 1973

Given their differences — in style, sensibility, aesthetic ideology and artistic practices — it is rather remarkable that in the 1960s both Andy Warhol and Sol LeWitt, paradigms of the Pop Artist and Conceptual Artist respectively, shared the desire to model their artistic practices on the machine. What made the machine so attractive as an object of imitation?

Of course the easiest answer is that being a machine was a way *not* to be Abstract Expressionist. The rhetoric of the machine was ready-made for the aesthetic-ideological work of negating the perceived humanism and romanticism of Abstract Expressionism because it aggressively references the rationalized and alienating mode of labor which had been for most of the century the exact opposite of "art." Imitating the machine enabled LeWitt and Warhol to change their art historical referent from Abstract Expressionism towards "non-composition," an anti-art tradition that can be traced back to Duchamp and the Russian avant-garde. The noncompositional task involves finding an ordering principle for one's art or literature that depends as little as possible (ideally not at all) on subjective choice, where a pregiven system — a machine — produces the art-work in a way that erases one's own subjectivity and individuality.[1]

Artists' baldly proclaimed and widely publicized embrace of the machine in the 1960s carried with it the danger of appearing to affirm post-war industrial society, and the new forms of labor, organization, mass culture and the commodity that characterized it. Everyday life, the argument would go, has *already* turned us into machines, as consumers of mass produced commodities and culture and as workers. Art, then, should help us reconnect with what is human and creative, not underscore our subjection to the machine. The notion of the person-as-machine conjures up images of workers on the assembly line. Marx summed up the position well: "In handicrafts and manufacture, the worker makes use of a tool; in the factory, the machine makes use of him. . . . In the factory we have a lifeless mechanism which is independent of the workers, who are incorporated into it as living appendages."[2] And modern designers of the factory did, in fact, think of the human body as a machine. In his influential 1911 study, *The Principles of Scientific Management*, F.W. Taylor argued that a radical increase in the efficiency of work processes could be achieved by conducting rigorous time and motion studies of each part of the labor process. Once the most efficient bodily movements were determined, they would establish a standard that the "scientific manager" would teach and enforce.[3] Henry Ford implemented and expanded Taylor's insights in his automobile factories, more or less institutionalizing the assembly line and the repetitive motions it required from workers as the basis of modern industrial production.

However, it is worth remembering that before the 1960s, the main contexts in which it seemed possible to bring the machine into art-making were the explicitly anti-capitalist ones of Soviet Constructivism and the Bauhaus. In those movements, the artist took the machine out of the Taylorized, Fordist factory and put it in the context of art in an attempt to reinvent the machine, to insist that the machine and mechanicalness were not inherently alienating. (The poet Vladimir Mayakovsky, for example, could speak of his "machine-parts" in proclaiming: "I myself feel like a Soviet factory, manufacturing happiness."[4]) Machine-like art and poetry shared with the autonomous art that it paralleled the sense that art was a space for saving subjectivity from the alienat-

1.
On noncomposition see Howard Singerman, "The Effects of Non-Composition," in *La Part de l'Oeil*, Brussels, 2000. Also see Yve-Alain Bois, "Les Annees Supports/Surfaces," *Artforum* 37, no. 4 (December 1988).
2.
Karl Marx, *Capital: A Critique of Political Economy*, vol. 1, trans. Ben Fowkes (New York: Penguin Books, 1976), p. 548.
3.
F.W. Taylor, *The Principles of Scientific Management* (New York: Norton, 1967). Also see David Harvey on the Taylorist and Fordist projects in David Harvey, *The Condition of Postmodernity* (Cambridge: Basil Blackwell, 1989).
4.
In the 1925 poem "Back Home!" ("*Domoy*"), *The Bedbug and Selected Poetry* trans. Max Hayward and George Reavey (Bloomington: Indiana University Press, 1975), pp. 186-7. Also see Christina Lodder, *Constructivism* (New Haven: Yale University Press, 1983) for more on Constructivism's rich and complicated relationship to the machine.

ing forces of modernization, a space for experimenting with alternative modernities. The Constructivist reconceptualization of the role of the artist along technological lines was part of an effort to figure out how the artist could play a role in the creation of a non-capitalist modernity. In her study of the "machine in the studio" Caroline Jones makes the case that those political motivations had more or less evaporated by the 1960s when artists like Frank Stella, Warhol and Robert Smithson started not only to represent the machine but to imitate it.[5] While it does seem clear, as Jones writes, that "postwar industrial capitalism inhabited the consciousness" of these artists and "motivated the making of their art,"[6] this "inhabiting" and "motivation" does not necessarily imply affirmation. Neither Warhol nor LeWitt ever embraced the explicitly political stance of a movement like Soviet Constructivism, not least because they lacked the revolutionary social context. However, this lack of explicit alignment with a political movement does not make their work any less critical a response to the world in which they lived. In fact, both Warhol and LeWitt hold open a space for critique and opposition. For those who experience the particular melancholy of the revolutionary in non-revolutionary times, the artwork of LeWitt and Warhol, I will argue, offer two very different kinds of assistance.

The advantages of examining Warhol and LeWitt together here are several. Their juxtaposition puts them each into a different context and thus helps to render both of them newly unfamiliar. While Warhol and LeWitt are each interested in the machine in a highly idiosyncratic way, it is precisely by looking at these two idiosyncratic ways of seeing the world in relation to each other that we can best appreciate not only their singularity but also the historical situation that they share.

In my effort to understand what the art of Warhol and LeWitt is saying about the world in which they lived, my central question will be: what is the emotional context, the historical mood, in which the aesthetic experience offered to viewers in the work of Warhol and LeWitt is attractive? My presumption here is that the affective nature of aesthetic experience is always at least partly compensatory. In other words, the experience of art has an emotional force because it offers us something in the space of "art" that we do not get elsewhere. Art is, in this view, always partly utopian. Of course, utopias are always also a critique of the world in which they appear. Every aesthetic experience (in giving us something that is otherwise missing) provides a picture of the world from which it has sprung. But it does so in reverse, like a photographic negative. And each artwork has its own way of seeing (its own "theory" of) the world. Each has its own relationship to the aggregate of shifting, competing and contradictory forces that shape everyday life. The task of the critic, then, is to reconstruct this world — which we might also call "history" — in order to make sense of the attractions of the specific experience that the artwork offers. This reconstruction must start from the aesthetic experience that the art promotes because it is precisely here, on the level of affect, I will contend, that we can most clearly see the residue of historicity. Subjective affect is the shuttle on which history gets into art and also how it comes back. So when I say (as I will) that LeWitt's and Warhol's art contains within it an implicit theory of the historical situation, by "history," I do not mean "historical events," or what is sometimes called the "linear history" that is offered in textbooks. History in the sense I am using it is not "there"

in any immediately observable way. Rather, history is only conceivable as an absent cause.[7] It is the set of problems in relation to which a given practice is attractive and interesting. My claim is that one way to access Warhol's and LeWitt's critique of and utopian response to their world is in their engagement with the machine and machine-ness.

I will argue that the idea of the machine provides the site through which Warhol and LeWitt are able to mediate — to represent and transform, to reproduce and allegorize — two related historical processes. The first, mentioned above, is the Taylorization of labor: the treatment of the human body as a machine, an instrument, in order to increase the body's efficiency in the context of industrial labor. This instrumentalization of the human body of course was not limited to the factory context, and was broadly perceived by the post-war period to

5.
Caroline Jones, *The Machine In the Studio: Constructing the Postwar American Artist* (Chicago; University of Chicago Press, 1996). Jones makes a helpful distinction between iconic and performative referencing of the mechanical. The representation is iconic, she writes, when "an image, figure, or representation that is somehow indexed to technology, to the industrial order or to the machine," p. 55. The performative is defined as "a mode of production that aspires to, or structurally resembles, an industrial process, and/or a self-presentation on the part of the artist that implies a collaboratively generated technological solution or mechanistic goal," p. 55. Jones argues that while the use of the machine as an icon in works of art is a widely deployed trope in modernism, the attempt to model one's compositional practices on the machine distinguishes postwar American artists like Stella, Warhol and Smithson from the artists that preceded them. "American artists of the 1960s effected a union of the iconic and performative, attempting to offer a kind of sublimity in the both the technological look, and the quasi-industrial production of their art," p. 55.
6.
Jones, *The Machine In the Studio*, p. 359.
7.
On history as an absent cause, see Fredric Jameson, *The Political Unconscious* (Ithaca: Cornell University Press, 1981), especially pp. 23 – 58.

8.
Niklas Luhmann, *The Differentiation of Society*. Translated by Stephen Holmes and Charles Larmore. (New York: Columbia University Press, 1982.)

9.
Niklas Luhmann, "Modernity in Contemporary Society," *Observations on Modernity* (Stanford: Stanford University Press, 1998), p. 1.

10.
Luhmann, "Modernity," p. 6.

11.
Luhmann, *Differentiation of Society*, p. 230.

12.
For more on systems theory see William Rasch and Cary Wolfe, "Introduction: Systems Theory and the Politics of Postmodernity," *Observing Complexity: Systems Theory and Postmodernity* (Minneapolis, University of Minnesota Press, 2000. Also see Steven Joshua Heims, *Constructing a Social Science for Postwar America: The Cybernetics Group, 1946 — 1953.* (Cambridge: MIT Press, 1993); and Eve Kosofsky Sedgwick and Adam Frank, "Shame in the Cybernetic Fold: Reading Silvan Tomkins," *Shame and Its Sisters: A Silvan Tomkins Reader* (Durham: Duke University Press, 1995).

13.
Gilles Deleuze and Felix Guattari, *Anti-Oedipus: Capitalism and Schizophrenia* (New York: Penguin, 1977), p. 6.

14.
Deleuze and Guattari, *Anti-Oedipus*, p. 6.

15.
See note 7.

16.
Luhmann, *Differentiation of Society*, p. 249.

have penetrated many areas of American life, including the life of the professional-managerial class. The second process (one that is closely related to the first) is what the German sociologist Niklas Luhmann has called the "differentiation of society." By this he means (and here I simplify) the division of society into different autonomous subsystems all of which have their own logic and function: civil society, law, medicine, the economy, art, and so on.[8] We might call this development the systematization of the lifeworld, but a systematization that works not according to a single logic, but one in which there are multiple systems each with their own logic. To live in this world not only requires that we learn the internal logic and procedures of multiple systems, but that we learn to negotiate among them as well. Before examining this idea further, however, it might help to explore exactly what I mean by "system" here.

flux, from the point of view of the energy that flows from it: the eye interprets everything — speaking, understanding, shitting, fucking — in terms of seeing."[13] Because the reason for the system's coming into being is precisely to cope with an environment, to simplify it and make it manageable, all systems are always interacting with other ones. By definition, although the system is totalizing and monologic in its own space, it is never singular: "one machine is always coupled with another . . . a connection with another machine is always established, along a transverse path, so that one machine interrupts the current of the other or "sees" its own current interrupted."[14] Here, I can provisionally state my argument about LeWitt and Warhol: where Warhol is interested in this moment of system coupling or system interface, LeWitt is concerned with the construction of systems themselves; his art duplicates and abstracts the pleasures of "a reduction of complexity that can be constructed and realized even though the world and the society where this takes place is unknown."[15]

A system, Luhmann writes, is a way to reduce "infinite to finite information loads."[9] The system achieves this through a form of "functional simplification . . . a reduction of complexity that can be constructed and realized even though the world and the society where this takes place is unknown."[10] I propose that we understand the "machine" in both LeWitt and Warhol to mean this moment of "functional simplification." "Systems theory," Luhmann writes, "supplanted the classical model of a whole made out of parts and relations between parts with a model emphasizing the difference between systems and environments."[11] The foundational gesture of the system is to distinguish an inside (the system) from an outside (the environment) and to setup a "feedback mechanism" or "feedback loop" for dealing with that environment. Feedback describes the process whereby the results of an act (output) are fed back (as input) to modify the initial act.[12] The thermostat is a common example of a feedback mechanism. The thermostat is the mechanism by which the system regulates itself, tests the results of its acts (the turning on or off of the furnace) and takes it back in as information to determine what to do next (the turning on or off of the furnace).

The thermostat, like any feedback mechanism, does its work by seeing everything else — the "environment" — only on the terms relevant to the system; nothing about the world matters to the thermostat except the temperature, which is indeed a reduction of infinite information loads to quite finite ones. Systems are monologic: they see the entire world in their own terms. Or as Deleuze and Guattari have put it, but speaking now of *human* physiological systems: "Doubtless each organ-machine interprets the entire world from the point of view of its own

But if my claim is that systems are interesting to Warhol and LeWitt because they allow them to mediate the historical situation, I need now to describe that situation. "Functional differentiation," Luhmann writes, "leads to a condition in which the genesis of problems and the solution to problems fall asunder. Problems can no longer be solved by the system that produces them. They have to be transferred to the system that is best equipped and specialized to solve them."[16] Each subsystem has to be ready to deal with problems generated out of its sphere. Life is less and less determined by local contexts as the local system context — whether it is the family, or the city, or medicine, or a particular profession or the legal system — is always responding to problems produced somewhere else. While each system has increased "autonomy" — *ie* an ability to apply "specific rules and procedures to special problems" — it also has decreased "autarchy" *ie* less and less authority outside of its own subsystem, and less of an ability to decide *what* problems it would be dealing with.[17] The increased autonomy can produce a false sense of confidence in the efficaciousness of one's own operations. Modernism could be seen as the recurring moment of misrecognition whereby each system operates as if it can and should solve the world's problems. Modernist legal theory, economics, international relations (think of the League of Nations), linguistics (the invention of Esperanto) and of course literature and art — are all colored with a strong redemptive strain.

There is a strong tradition wherein art is understood as a space that can redeem, repair, or at least offer a temporary

hiding place (for artist and viewer) from a depressing world, from that thing in the world from which one wants to escape: whether it is means-ends rationality, reification, misogyny, homophobia, racism or another oppressive social force. The critique of this idea of autonomous art has been that it is essentially compensatory, and therefore affirmative of the order of things. That "art develops its own strategies to satisfy needs that originate in other realms of social interaction"[18] prevents people from trying to actually change these other realms of social interaction. It was against this idea of art as a separate sphere that the historical avant-garde — the Russian futurists, dada and surrealism — reacted.[19] The idea was that if you destroyed art, then all those creative energies that were being wasted in the sphere of art would be released into the world. Hence the avant-garde slogan: "Art into Life."

As a rejoinder to the avant-gardiste desire to sublate art into life, Luhmann might point out that there are not just two systems 'art' and 'life,' but multiple systems, and dissolving one opposition does not overthrow the entire aggregate. Indeed, the differentiation of society makes opposition difficult, because inasmuch as we are always seeing the world from within a system at any given time, it is impossible to have a total picture of all the systems. This is a major distinction from the whole – parts model of society; here, there is no holistic logic, there is no unified system organizing the systems. One thing this means is that there is inevitably a contradiction between "a phenomenological description of the life of an individual and a more properly structural model of the conditions of existence of that experience"[20] because that overall structural model is impossible to attain. This contradiction between the experience of everyday life and the possibility of describing the transpersonal, historical forces that make that everyday experience possible has become endemic. As such it constitutes a basic problem for *any* attempt to represent the world. LeWitt and Warhol offer quite different responses to the problem created by this contradiction, but they are both, I argue, preoccupied with it. In sum, I am suggesting that the insights of systems theory provide us with the conceptual vocabulary to reconstruct the world that is implied by the work of Warhol and LeWitt. I contend that the attractions of their art as well as the significance of their differences make more sense when we presume that the world structured by what Luhmann calls "functional differentiation" is their context.

Warhol's Pop represents a move away from autonomous art. For Warhol, there is not going to be any redemption going on in any one system: art is not going to save the world. Instead, Warhol poaches on already existing spaces (the art world, the artist's studio, cinema, advertising, mass culture) to create alternative spaces in which he can set himself to the task of learning how to imagine and inhabit system interfaces.[21] The Warholian task is basically to study, to figure out and work with the internal logic of each of these subsystems, and to imagine and to experiment with different moments of system coupling. What I want to discuss next is how this moment of interface was especially promising for Warhol because it enabled him and his audience to perceive likenesses, which, I will argue, was for Warhol the condition of possibility for liking things. That for Warhol to be a machine was to be coupled with other machines, and that this was for him the locus of emotional attachment and liking, is indicated by the fact that Warhol for many years carried

17.
Ibid.
18.
Jochen Schulte-Sasse, "Afterword: Can the Imagination be Mimetic under Conditions of Modernity?" in Luiz Costa Lima, *Control of the Imaginary: Reason and Imagination in Modern Times* (Minneapolis: University Of Minnesota Press, 1988), p. 215.
19.
The classic formulation of this argument can be found in Peter Burger, *The Theory of the Avant-garde* trans. Michael Shaw (Minneapolis: University of Minnesota Press, 1984). I take the term "historical avant-garde" from Burger.
20.
Fredric Jameson, *Postmodernism, or the Cultural Logic of Late Capital*, (Durham, Duke University Press, 1990), p. 410.
21.
In "Warhol Gives Good Face: Publicity and the Politics of Prosopopoiea," *Pop Out: Queer Warhol* ed. Jennifer Doyle, Jonathan Flatley, José Muñoz, (Durham: Duke University Press, 1996), I argue that Warhol created queer versions of what Nancy Fraser has called "subaltern counterpublics." See Fraser, "Rethinking the Public Sphere: A Contribution to the Critique of Actually Existing Democracy," in *The Phantom Public Sphere* ed. Bruce Robbins (Minneapolis: University of Minnesota Press, 1993).

around a tape recorder he referred to as "his wife" (fig. 1).

LeWitt, on the other hand, is more concerned with the nominalistic pleasures of systematicity as such. His systems-based wall drawings and serial works alike reproduce in an abstracted form the moment of "functional simplification," that "reduction of complexity that can be constructed and realized even though the world and the society where this takes place is unknown." Within the aesthetic experience itself, LeWitt restages the above-mentioned contradiction between everyday experience and a structural model of the conditions of possibility of that experience. This aesthetic experience is characterized by a tension between the visual perception of his work and the cognitive comprehension of the structural concept organizing the work. Much (although of course not all) of LeWitt's work dramatizes this difference between comprehension and perception. LeWitt thereby takes the contradiction produced by autonomous, *competing* systems (that preclude a view of the totality of systems) — abstracts it into an aesthetic feeling — and encompasses this itself *into* a system. In *Variations of Incomplete Open Cubes*, LeWitt duplicates and defamiliarizes the social fact of this contradiction and at the same time shows us what the resolution of this contradiction would feel like, since the total organizing concept is there, even if it is in tension with its own material manifestation. This move takes on

additional critical force, I will contend, inasmuch as mass culture and the commodity present the world as if everyday life is more or less in harmony with the social order as a whole, as if the particular is always happily made meaningful by the universal. If LeWitt's work interrupts this illusion of harmony between the particular with the general, it has a more utopian side as well, reproducing as an abstract feeling what Luhmann argues is the best we can hope for: to engage imaginatively and creatively with the possibilities of combination between different systems. This is what Luhmann calls "the unity of the imaginary space of [a system's] own combinatory potentials."[22] After all, "and all of its combinations" is one of LeWitt's favorite ways to build a system (fig. 2).

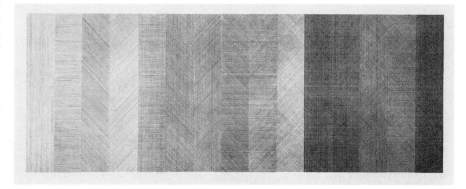

22.
Luhmann, "Modernity," p. 10.

IMITATION

CHILDREN'S PLAY IS EVERYWHERE PERMEATED BY MIMETIC MODES OF BEHAVIOR, AND ITS REALM IS BY NO MEANS LIMITED TO WHAT ONE PERSON CAN IMITATE IN ANOTHER. THE CHILD PLAYS AT BEING NOT ONLY A SHOPKEEPER OR TEACHER BUT ALSO A WINDMILL OR A TRAIN.
— Walter Benjamin[23]

Like many of Warhol's aphoristic assertions, his statement that he wanted to be machine has a simplicity of diction that belies the number of symbolic strands and social desires and anxieties that it catches up. Warhol is speaking first of all about the way that he is "painting the way he does." His painting is machine-like because he uses the silkscreening technique, which employs a repetitive, mechanical method and which relies on a mechanically-produced photograph-derived image as a model.[24] The silkscreening process is automatic, predictable and technologically mediated; it eliminates traces of the author's hand while nonetheless preserving a kind of accidental mechanical variation. Silkscreening also means that the paintings can in principle be produced by anybody: like products off an assembly line, they are both anonymously and collaboratively produced. "I think it would be so great," Warhol said, "if more people took up silk screens so that no one would know whether my picture was mine or somebody else's."[25] The "assembly line effect" of the silkscreens, along with the naming of his studio as the Factory, together underscored the extent to which Warhol appeared to be referencing the historical form of rationalized, Taylorized labor itself, and indeed to be colluding with it.

Warhol was also painting in a machine-like way inasmuch as he tried to paint without thinking or choosing: "When I have to think about it, I know the picture is wrong. . . . My instinct about painting says. 'if you don't think about it, its right.' As soon as you have to decide and choose, it's wrong. And the more you decide about the more wrong it gets."[26] The *Do It Yourself* series (fig. 3), which Warhol produced just before he started silkscreening, offers a self-reflexive allegory of this desire. Not only is Warhol painting (or drawing) according to a preset plan that involves no choice or thought, it is a preset plan that is mass produced — that is, itself produced off an assembly line according to a preset plan. In a sense, all of Warhol's paintings were *Do It Yourself* works inasmuch as they are paintings of precisely those images that anyone could paint because everyone knows them, images that were *already* produced. No one could accuse Warhol of creativity or subjectivity when he painted commodity labels, celebrities, advertisements, newspaper photos or dollar bills. Warhol painted the images that were already there in everyone's consciousness automatically as an effect of repetition, without thinking — the things that everyone saw everyday. In this sense Warhol's painting was indexical; he was like a machine for recording what was around him. And his fascination with an automatic, non-subjective recording of the world was by no means limited to painting: film, photography, audio tapes, video — Warhol wanted to mediate his world through as many machines as he could as frequently as possible.

While Warhol's clear affinity for the machine helped to solidify the critical and popular perception that Warhol was affectless and "asexual," I think that it is precisely in and around the "machine-like" that we will find Warhol's emotions and

FIG.3

Andy Warhol
Do It Yourself (Flowers), 1962
Colored crayon on paper
25 x 18"
Courtesy of Sonnabend Gallery
Copyright The Andy Warhol
Foundation for
the Visual Arts/ARS

23.
Walter Benjamin, "Doctrine of the Similar," *Walter Benjamin: Selected Writings, Vol. 2* ed. Michael Jennings (Cambridge: Harvard University Press, 1999), p. 694.

24.
On the silkscreen, Warhol says: "You pick a photograph, blow it up, transfer it in glue onto silk, and then roll ink across it so the ink goes through the silk but not through the glue. That way you get the same image, slightly different each time. It was all so simple — quick and chancy. I was thrilled with it" (Andy Warhol and Pat Hackett, *POPism: The Warhol Sixities* [New York: Harcourt, Brace, Jovanovich, 1980], p. 22).

25.
Andy Warhol, "What Is Pop Art?" interview by G.R. Swenson, *Art News*, Volume 62, Number 7, (November 1963): p. 26.

26.
Andy Warhol, *The Philosophy of Andy Warhol from A to B and Back Again* (New York: Harcourt, Brace, Jovanovich, 1975), p. 149.

desires. For Warhol, the machine does not signal the negation of affect, but the condition of possibility for affective attachment, pleasure and desire. In the area of affect and desire we find Warhol's resistance to and perversion of the Taylorist body-machine system. Take, for example, one of my favorite Warhol anecdotes from *POPism*: "During this period [1969] I took thousands of Polaroids of genitals. Whenever somebody came up to the Factory, no matter how straight looking he was, I'd ask him to take his pants off so I could photograph his cock and balls. It was surprising who'd let me and who wouldn't."[27] The mediation of the camera at once emboldened Warhol to ask men to show their genitalia and allowed men to display them. It allowed men to think that the display was after all not so much for Warhol the person so much as it was "for the camera." For Warhol, thinking about the world in terms of its photographability opened up new worlds, quite literally changing what he saw and how he saw it. And it changed how people related to him. The camera opens up new possibilities. In short, for Warhol technological mediation would always be a huge turn-on.

That the point of Warhol's machine-like mediated world is not detachment or emotionlessness, but sexiness and emotional investment is also suggested by a work like *Dance Floor Diagram* (fig. 4). The diagram puts to use the same rationalization of bodily movements that made the assembly line possible. But here the ability of the body to move automatically according to a preset system is the condition of possibility not for efficient work but for learning to dance, which suggests that work and pleasure are not necessarily opposed.[28] Both are machine-like. Indeed, in the instance of the dance diagram, the imitation of the machine can lead to emotional attachment to, and desire for, other people.

This is not to say that Warhol was unattuned to the ways that machines were fundamentally indifferent to human life. In the context of the car crash (fig. 5) and electric chair paintings, Warhol's assertion that he wants to be a machine reads like an ironic rewriting of Whitman's "singing the body electric." Advocating a machine utopia he was not. In a way, the car crash paintings are the flip side of the dance step diagrams. Each are equally distant from an affirmation of the industrial factory, the one pointing to the unexpected non-industrial uses and pleasures of bodily rationalization, the other to the machine — and precisely the machine that was produced on the Fordist assembly line — as an instrument of death. Together, these paintings suggest that we pay more attention to moments when we interface with machines and when we ourselves seem to be machine-like. The message would seem to be that machine-ness — indifferent to human life as it may be — can no longer be thought of as the limit of the human, the opposite of the human.

Indeed, being machine-like is what enables us to do something so basic as liking things and people. In the following 1963 interview, Warhol discusses his affinity for the machine at some length.

27.
Warhol and Hackett, *POPism*, p. 294.
28.
Warhol also liked to insist that sex is hard work,
see Warhol, *Philosophy*, p. 97.

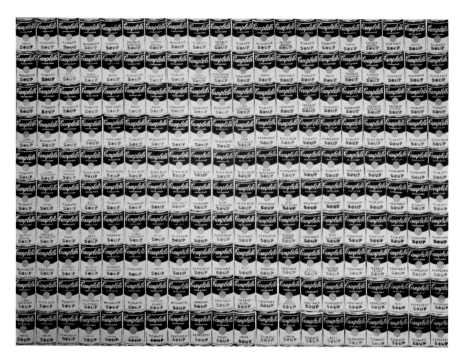

WARHOL:

SOMEONE SAID THAT BRECHT WANTED EVERYBODY TO THINK ALIKE. I WANT EVERYBODY TO THINK ALIKE. BUT BRECHT WANTED TO DO IT THROUGH COMMUNISM, IN A WAY. RUSSIA IS DOING IT UNDER GOVERNMENT. IT'S HAPPENING HERE ALL BY ITSELF WITHOUT BEING UNDER A STRICT GOVERNMENT; SO, IF IT'S WORKING WITHOUT TRYING, WHY CAN'T IT WORK WITHOUT BEING COMMUNIST? EVERYBODY LOOKS ALIKE AND ACTS ALIKE, AND WE'RE GETTING MORE AND MORE THAT WAY.

I THINK EVERYBODY SHOULD BE A MACHINE.

I THINK EVERYBODY SHOULD LIKE EVERYBODY.

SWENSON:

IS THAT WHAT POP ART IS ALL ABOUT?

WARHOL:

YES. IT'S LIKING THINGS.

SWENSON:

AND LIKING THINGS IS LIKE BEING A MACHINE?

WARHOL:

YES, BECAUSE YOU DO THE SAME THING EVERY TIME. YOU DO IT OVER AND OVER AGAIN. [29]

29.
Swenson interview, p. 26.

Here, by playing with the slide between "like" in its transitive sense (to like something) and in its intransitive, prepositional use (to be like something), Warhol appears to be making the connection between three things: the perception of likeness, the desire to be alike, and the act of liking. The logic is something like the following. Brecht wanted everyone to think alike through Communism. In the United States (like in Russia, under Communism), everybody "looks and acts alike." Here, as if it follows logically from everybody *being* alike, Warhol makes the key association of the interview: Warhol wants everybody to be a machine and he wants everybody to like everybody. The suggestion made through a chain of association (everybody being alike, everybody being a machine, everybody liking everybody) is that *being* alike somehow sets the stage for *liking*; to like something or somebody, one has to be able to feel likeness at the basis of the connection. *Liking* is like *being* alike. And liking things, that's what Pop is, which is "like being a machine," because it is doing the same thing every time. And here, repetition enters the scene with a kind of explanatory promise: repetition, Warhol asserts, which we might think of as the production of likenesses, is also like liking. The sets of associations are rather dizzying, if pleasurably so. How can we make sense of the connections among likeness, liking, machine-likeness and repetition?

Before examining the connection between being like and liking, it might help to consider what it might mean to "be like" something else, to be *similar* to something else rather than the *same* as it. Warhol's use of repetition shows us that it is not identity in which Warhol is interested (fig. 6). Serial repetition itself destabilizes sameness, producing instead what Foucault calls "similitude." In the

FIG.6

Andy Warhol
Two Hundred Campbell's Soup Cans, 1962
Synthetic polymer paint and silkscreen
ink on canvas
6' x 8'4"
Copyright The Andy Warhol Foundation for the Visual Arts/ARS

final lines of his short book on Magritte, Foucault writes: "A day will come when, by means of similitude relayed indefinitely along the length of a series, the image itself, along with the name it bears, will lose its identity. Campbell, Campbell, Campbell, Campbell."[30] What Foucault is getting at is the fact that the machine does not represent, it imitates, or perhaps more exactly: it simulates.[31] When Warhol paints the soup cans, he is not trying to "represent" them; the painting is not referential in this sense – it is not providing us with a window onto the world. It is not a painting "of" 200 Campbell soup cans. Rather, Warhol is mechanically simulating the image of the can, based on a model. Whereas re-presentation means the thing is *not* here, it negates the thing represented, simulation involves a repeated effort to be like the model. Warhol seems to have liked the mistakes that are built into the silkscreening process itself (seen more clearly in the car crash paintings), the differences that were accidental, in part because they emphasize the similitude – the non-identity – of the images.

What, however, does likeness have to do with *liking*? Here the German critic Walter Benjamin, who sustained a lifelong interest in the importance of "similarity," is helpful. Benjamin is interested in "likeness" precisely to the extent that we are less and less able to perceive it. This ability has declined because the systems of equivalence set up by a money economy tend to obscure the more subtle quality of similarity. Living in a world in which anything can be exchanged for anything else via the abstraction of money encourages us to think in terms of the binary opposition identity/difference. The more subtle antennae of what Benjamin calls the "mimetic faculty" wither away in this context. The decline in the mimetic faculty is a problem in Benjamin's view because he believed that the perception of similarity was the key to emotional attachment. Think, for example, of the importance of the returned smile. So many facial gestures are precisely about this confirmation of likeness — if someone smiles, we smile back. If someone is frowning, we frown. Fear can produce fear. Watching a yawn makes yawning nearly irresistible. Towards the beginning of the century there were a series of studies which discovered what is called the "Carpenter effect": this tells us that in fact these responses were involuntary, machine-like: we automatically mimic the facial expressions of others. Imitation forms the basic tissue of relationality.[32] For Benjamin, and here we are back to Warhol, the ability to be like is the precondition for liking.

That this mimetic faculty was still present in children was cause, for Benjamin, for hope. "Children's play is everywhere permeated by mimetic modes of behavior, and its realm is by no means limited to what one person can imitate in another. The child plays at being not only a shopkeeper or teacher but also a windmill or a train." The mimetic capacity of children, in other words, is so vital, that they even play at *being machines*. The child does not perceive the machine in the industrial context, but simply as another thing to imitate. And this behavior is itself rather machine-like inasmuch as imitation is itself mechanical, indexical, acting according to a preset form. Benjamin sees children as imitation machines. Benjamin, like Warhol then, wishes to reverse the notion that we start out as "human" and then through our encounter with machines become dehumanized. Rather, we are always already machine-like. Indeed, we start out *more* machine like. When we get into trouble is when we forget this fact in our reification of the human-machine opposition and put "imitation" on the machine side as something to be avoided. Benjamin, like Warhol, hoped to help us remember how to be machine-like, which is to say how to be like, and he hoped that the new technologies of photography and film — insofar as they could be divorced from an industrial context — could help us in this task.

The new technologies are able to help in the invigorating of the mimetic faculty precisely because of their systemic quality, because each technology is in essence "a functional simplification, that is, a form of the reduction of complexity that can be constructed and realized." Each technology affords its own particular way of seeing the world. Just as it is a different nature that speaks to the thermostat (a nature defined by temperature alone), it is also, as Benjamin said, "a different nature that

30.
Michel Foucault, *This is Not a Pipe*, (Berkeley: University of California Press, 1981), p. 54.
31.
Simulation owes its critical currency as a term to Jean Baudrillard, who wrote apropos simulation: "Here it is a question of a reversal of origin and finality, for all the forms change once they are not so much mechanically reproduced but *conceived from the point-of-view of the their very reproducibility*, diffracted from a generating nucleus we call the model." Jean Baudrillard, *Simulations* (New York: Semiotext(e), 1983), p. 100. For comment on Warhol specifically see pp. 136, 144, and 158-9.
32.
I take this example, and a sense of the centrality of the mimetic faculty in Benjamin's thinking from Miriam Hansen's "Benjamin and Cinema: Not a One Way Street" in *Critical Inquiry* 25, no. 2 (Winter, 1999). See pp. 317-8 and pp. 329-332 in particular.

speaks to the camera than to the human eye."[33] On one level, Benjamin is speaking of things like the motion studies of Muybridge, where the camera records specifics of bodily movement which are invisible to the naked eye. But he is also describing the way that in the process of translation from one system to another, the moment of coupling between machines, what is conveyed is not an equivalence, but a similitude. To get a better sense of how this works, think of translation between languages: everyone knows that two words that "mean the same thing" in different languages do not really mean in the same way, they have different connotations, shades of meaning, histories: "bread," the French "*pain*," the Russian "*khlyeb*." They are similar but not the same. Linguistic translation requires the operations of the mimetic faculty.

But, it is not only linguistic translation that requires the perception of similarity. For example, when the face is translated onto the movie screen it is also translated into something else, what we might call a simulation of the face. Warhol understood this, which is why he would give screen tests: "That screen magnetism is something secret — if you could only figure out what it is and how to make it, you'd have a really good product to sell. But you can't even tell if someone has it until you actually see them up there on the screen. You have to give screen tests to find out."[34] You recognize Edie's or Baby Jane's face up there, but our mode of looking when we're looking at a moving image projected on a screen is quite different from the one when we see someone face to face (fig. 7). Screen beauty is different from life beauty. And some people have screen magnetism and others do not. In the process of translation between systems the mimetic faculty is invoked, and this is why Benjamin is so

hopeful about the possibilities of technology for changing the possibilities of our mimetic capacities. Creative mistranslations, distorted resemblances — these can jump start the mimetic faculty because they force us to take conscious notice of what we are doing. To make any connection we have to think in terms of similarity; we are forced out of the identity — difference dichotomy. Or, in Warhol's terms, these moments of system interface enable the perception of likeness, which is necessary if everybody is to like everybody, as Warhol thinks they should.

Warhol's interest with system interface can be seen throughout his career. For example, in 1976 he acquired a Minox 35 El, and it was this camera (or other small SLRs like it) that he carried with him everywhere for the rest of his life, replacing his "wife" that had earlier been his constant companion. It has been estimated that he took on average a roll of film every day for the rest of his life.[35] Warhol loved to talk on the phone and watch TV at the same time. The more machine-mediation the better. Like the camera, the telephone changes the nature of relationality. We all know that some things are easier to hear or to say on the phone. Warhol's interest in system interface is also why Warhol liked to have his assistants misunderstand him a little bit:

33.
"A Little History of Photography," *Walter Benjamin: Selected Writings, Vol. 2* (Cambridge: Harvard University Press, 1999), p. 510.
34.
Warhol, *Philosophy*, p. 63.
35.
Mark Francis writes "Over his last decade, from 1976 to 1986, it is likely that Warhol exposed at least one roll of film a day on average." In Mark Francis, "Still Life: Andy Warhol's Photography as a Form of Metaphysics," *Andy Warhol / Photography* (Zurich: Edition Stemmle, 1999) p. 23. There are more than 66,000 photographs in his estate.
36.
Warhol, *Philosophy*, p. 99.

FIG. 7

Andy Warhol
Screen Test: Jane Holzer, 1964
Film still
Copyright 2000 The Andy Warhol Museum, Pittsburgh, a museum of Carnegie Institute

SOMETHING THAT I LOOK FOR IN AN ASSOCIATE IS A CERTAIN AMOUNT OF MISUNDERSTANDING OF WHAT I'M TRYING TO DO. NOT A FUNDAMENTAL MISUNDERSTANDING; JUST MINOR MISUNDERSTANDINGS HERE AND THERE. WHEN SOMEONE DOESN'T QUITE COMPLETELY UNDERSTAND WHAT YOU WANT FROM THEM, OR WHEN THE TAPE IS BAD, OR WHEN THEIR OWN FANTASIES START COMING THROUGH, I OFTEN WIND UP LIKING WHAT COMES OUT OF IT ALL BETTER THAN I LIKED MY ORIGINAL IDEA. THEN IF YOU TAKE WHAT THE FIRST PERSON WHO MISUNDERSTOOD YOU DID, AND YOU GIVE THAT TO SOMEONE ELSE AND TELL THEM TO MAKE IT MORE LIKE HOW THEY KNOW YOU WOULD WANT IT, THAT'S GOOD TOO. IF PEOPLE NEVER MISUNDERSTAND YOU, AND IF THEY DO EVERYTHING EXACTLY THE WAY YOU TELL THEM TO, THEY'RE JUST TRANSMITTERS OF YOUR IDEAS, AND YOU GET BORED WITH THAT. BUT WHEN YOU WORK WITH PEOPLE WHO MISUNDERSTAND YOU, INSTEAD OF GETTING TRANSMISSIONS, YOU GET TRANSMUTATIONS, AND THAT'S MUCH MORE INTERESTING IN THE LONG RUN.[36]

When one's associate misunderstands, or "when the tape is bad," instead of transmissions, you get transmutations. The transmutation, rather than being an exact transmission or a metaphoric substitution is metonymic. It is a creative mistranslation. Like the party-game of telephone, it is better when people mis-hear, when their own fantasies come through.

This is the idea behind *A: a novel*, which is approximately 24 hours of conversation transcribed verbatim, in three sessions over the course of a couple years from 1965 to 1967. Reading *A* is nothing like listening to or participating in a conversation nor is it like reading the recorded speech in a novel. Because of its written quality, it is at once more tedious and more interesting to read. Meaning is hard to discern since the signifying work usually done by tone, facial expression, gesture when you are talking to someone face to face is left undone. So first, one notices these absences. And then other things begin to emerge — patterns, repetitions, correspondences, contradictions and incoherences — that are otherwise invisible when we are wrapped up in the logic of face to face interaction.

Warhol's interest in faces, in celebrity, in technologies of reproduction, in collect-

ing can all, I suggest, be productively thought about in terms of system interface, the (mis)translation between systems. The fact that this moment of system interface references the structure of feeling of the lifeworld in which we already live, a lifeworld defined by functional differentiation, is what gives Warhol's work its emotional punch. Warhol's work is essentially a primer for studying the production of likenesses and the liking that the inevitable coupling of systems enables. Warhol is reminding us that the moment of system translation is not just something *he* is doing, not just something that happens in "art," but a structuring principle of our everyday life-world, one that if avowed and used, has transformative potential because it can remind us how to like.

CONTRADICTION

THOSE WHO SUCCUMB TO THE IDEOLOGY ARE PRECISELY THOSE WHO COVER UP THE CONTRADICTION INSTEAD OF TAKING IT INTO THE CONSCIOUSNESS OF THEIR OWN PRODUCTION.
— Adorno and Horkheimer[37]

Like Warhol, LeWitt borrows the emotional force of his work from the fact we live in a world in which "life is determined less and less by local contexts," a world defined by the need for transition and translation between different systemic logics. But where Warhol is interested in creative mistranslations between systems, LeWitt's work, as I mentioned earlier, replicates — in the serial works as well as many of the wall drawings — the more nominalistic pleasure of reducing "infinite to finite information loads" by bringing the viewer into the world of a readily graspable systemic logic. LeWitt's work brings what Luhmann called the "unity of the imaginary space of combinatory potentials" *inside* the system. "Variation" and "combination" are two of LeWitt's favorite tropes, two of his most reliable ways to build systems. However, in works such as various as *Variations of Incomplete Open Cubes* and *All Combinations of Arcs from Corners and Sides; Straight Lines, Not-Straight-Lines and Broken Lines*, LeWitt brings the combinatory impulse, the generation of variations, into the work in a completely abstracted way, not directly referenceable to any social context. This gives the viewer a kind of abstract affective map of the combinatory experience. In this map, variation and combination always appear in relation to a total concept, a concept with which, however, variation is always also in a kind of tension. If being a machine for Warhol is about coupling with other machines, for LeWitt it is about duplicating for the viewer one element of life in a machine-like world. This element is the experience of a contradiction between the conceptual grasp of a total system and the particular perceptual experience of it.

Where for Warhol being a machine enables emotional attachment because it reminds us how to like, LeWitt sees his artwork as explicitly emotion*less*. Indeed he sees the avoidance of emotional expression as a major advantage of the conceptual approach. "Conceptual art is made to engage the mind of the viewer rather than his eye or emotions . . . It is the objective of the artist who is concerned with conceptual art to make his work conceptually interesting to the spectator, and therefore he would want it to become emotionally dry."[38] However, this does not mean that his work is not in some way about emotion; expression is not the only way to represent an emotion. LeWitt's work is "about" emotion and subjectivity precisely inasmuch as it negates these things.[39] As Adorno has put it: "There is no art that does not contain in itself as an element, negated, what it repulses. If it is more

37.
Max Horkheimer and Theodor Adorno, "The Culture Industry: Enlightenment as Mass Deception," *Dialectic of Enlightenment* trans. John Cumming, (New York: Continuum, 1972), p. 157.

38.
Sol LeWitt, "Paragraphs on Conceptual Art," in *Sol LeWitt: Critical Texts*, ed. Adachiara Zevi (Rome: I Libri di AEIOU), p. 78.

39.
Of course, the desire to combat romanticism and expressionism is one of the major strands of twentieth century art, a desire perhaps most famously expressed in T.S. Eliot's assertion: "Poetry is not a turning loose of emotion, but an escape from emotion; it is not the expression of personality, but an escape from personality. But of course only those who have personality and emotions know what it means to escape from those things" (T. S. Eliot, "Tradition and the Individual Talent," in *Selected Prose of T. S. Eliot*, ed. Frank Kermode [New York: Harcourt, Brace and Jovanovich, 1975], p. 43). This last sentence of Eliot's makes it clear that poetry here is still about emotion to the precise extent that it negates it. The unstated implication of Eliot's statement is that it is only in a world where one wants to escape from the emotions of everyday life — where those emotions are unpleasant — that this poetic gesture is attractive. For Eliot, this is a universal human condition — one *always* wants to escape from and transform emotion and personality in the realm of art. This is what makes life worth living. Of course, the universality of art-as-escape has been widely challenged in twentieth century art, not least by avant-garde movements like Surrealism, Dada, and Constructivism who sought to explode the creative energies to be found in "art into life." (Indeed, one might even read Eliot's own poetry as a critique of art-as-escape.) However, even if art is always about negation, the *particular* emotions that are worth escaping at a particular moment are widely variable and historically specific.

than mere indifference, the Kantian 'without interest' must be shadowed by the wildest interest, and there is much to be said for the idea that the dignity of artworks depends on the intensity of the interest from which they are wrested."[40] We can see the nature of the interest from which LeWittian disinterest is wrested by examining the specific quality of the aesthetic experience LeWitt's work offers.

IN 1967, relatively early on in LeWitt's career, artist and critic Mel Bochner provided an aptly prescient characterization of the aesthetic experience that LeWitt's work produces. "When one encounters a LeWitt, although an order is immediately intuited, how to apprehend or penetrate it is nowhere revealed. Instead one is overwhelmed with a mass of data — lines, joints, angles. By controlling so rigidly the conception of the work, never adjusting it to any predetermined ideas of how a work of art should look, LeWitt arrives at a unique perceptual breakdown of conceptual order into visual chaos."[41] Although Bochner was speaking of LeWitt's early serial structures (*Serial Project Set A* is his primary example, fig. 8), I think the characterization holds true not just for the serial works, but for many of the wall drawings as well. These are also often organized by a simple schema which is easily graspable conceptually — *Vertical Lines, Not Straight, Not Touching* (fig. 9) or *Ten thousand Lines, One Inch Long, Evenly Spaced on Six Walls each of*

Differing Area, for example — but perceptually overwhelming in their size and scope. The experience of a gap between apprehension (the sensory perception of the material object) and comprehension (the cognition of the total system organizing that material) would seem to be a recurring theme in LeWitt's art. As Tan Lin has recently argued, the effect bears a family resemblance to the optical illusion, where the mind imposes an underlying order which is contradicted by visual experience, leading you to see something that is not there.[42] Perhaps we could say that LeWitt's work operates like an *unraveled* optical illusion.[43] Here, visual experience and cognitive comprehension are collapsed but then held apart. This generates the effect not of illusion (where we see something that is not there) so much as of allegory (where representation operates across a gap). As I will discuss more below, the overall effect is one of surprise; viewing LeWitt's art, one is frequently surprised that such a simple concept could produce such an overwhelming visual experience.

Often, LeWitt's art actively assists the intuition of an overall order with language: *Lines Not Straight Not Touching, Five Cubes on 25 Squares, 10,000 lines five inches long*, and of course *Variations of Incomplete Open Cubes*, our primary topic here. If the title is insufficient or if one has not read it, LeWitt often provides a smaller, visually graspable version of the work. In the case of the large wall drawings, this takes the form of a smaller schematic drawing that accompanies the work (fig. 10). Or with the *Variations*, there is the overall schematic drawing (cat. 65, PAGE 13). Which is to say: while the work is often confusing, not to say stupefying on the local level, LeWitt's work generally provides easy access to the system from which this perceptual experience has been generated.

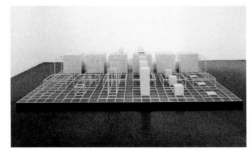

FIG.8

Sol LeWitt
Serial Project No. 1 (ABCD), 1966
Baked enamel on aluminum
Collection of The Museum of Modern Art, New York
Gift of Agnes Gund and purchase (by exchange)

FIG.9

Sol LeWitt
Wall Drawing #46 (Vertical lines, not straight, not touching, uniformly dispersed with maximum density, covering the entire surface of the wall) (detail), 1970
Black pencil
The LeWitt Collection, Chester, Connecticut

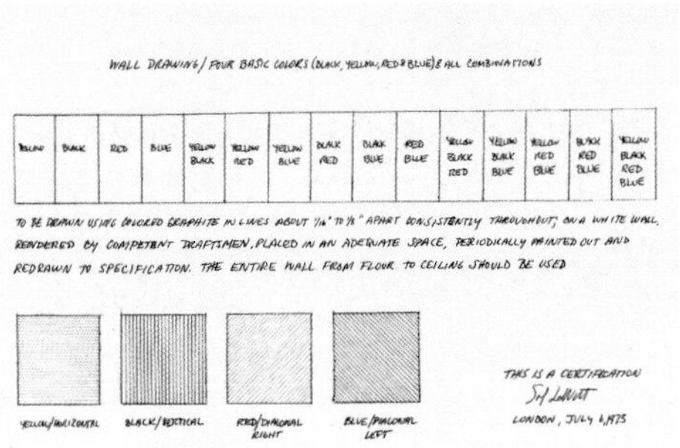

FIG.10

Sol LeWitt
Wall Drawing / Four Basic Colors (Black, Yellow, Red & Blue) & All Combinations, 1973
Original certification of wall drawing belonging to the Tate Gallery, London

40.
Theodor Adorno, *Aesthetic Theory*, trans. Robert Hullot-Kentor (Minneapolis: University of Minnesota Press, 1997), p. 11.
41.
"Serial Art, Systems, Solipsism," *Minimal Art: A Critical Anthology* ed. Gregory Battcock (New York: Dutton, 1968), p. 101.
42.
Tan Lin, "This Is A Novel or A aStopwatch," in *Elsewhere*, ed. Mary Ceruti (New York: Sculpture Center, 2000).
43.
I intend here to suggest a comparison with Foucault's argument about Magritte's work, which, Foucault argues, functions like an "unraveled calligram." Foucault, *This is Not a Pipe*.

44.
Sol LeWitt, "Commentaries," in *Sol LeWitt*, ed. Alicia Legg
(New York: The Museum of Modern Art, 1978), p. 81.
45.
LeWitt, *Sol LeWitt*, p. 81.
46.
Sol LeWitt, conversation with author and Nicholas Baume,
9 August 2000.

Part of the brilliance of *Variations of Incomplete Open Cubes* is its achievement of a particular, and particularly maximized, tension between perception and conception. The tension can be seen in the difficulty of executing the project. LeWitt writes that "although at first I thought it was not a complex project, this piece provided more problems than anticipated."[44] The idea was straightforward as a concept: a series constituted by all the possible variations of an open cube that was not complete. "The series started with three-part pieces because a cube implies three dimensions and, of course, ends with one eleven-part piece (one bar removed)."[45] The difficulty of the project lay in the task of figuring out all of the variations without duplicating them. Rotation here is the key formal problem since the same cube rotated often appears to be a different cube. In fact, despite LeWitt's persistent efforts, as the working drawings suggest, LeWitt discovered that rotating the incomplete cubes in one's head or in two dimensions proved to be impossible. "You can't construct the cubes in your mind, I find it impossible," LeWitt said. "I can't do it, and no one I know can do it."[46] LeWitt found that it was absolutely necessary to

make models — at first from pipe cleaners and paperclips — to figure it out.

The perceptual difficulty of the *Incomplete Open Cubes* may be related to the human tendency to perceive the incomplete open cube in terms of the complete cube. In other words, it is not that we complete the cube imaginatively in our head, but that a set of sometimes misleading perceptual truths about the complete open cube seem to infiltrate our perception of the incomplete ones. For example, it is surprising how difficult it is to move between two and three dimensions with the incomplete cubes. Because the complete cube looks the same from any angle, one is not prepared for the fact that, when drawn two dimensionally or photographed, the cube looks completely different depending on the angle it is seen from. Look, for example, at 8/12 and 8/13 in the artist's book (cat. 66) or in the photographic composite (cat. 67, PAGE 8): it is not, I think, immediately apparent that the two cubes, if presented from a different angle, are mirror images. The expectation of symmetry seems to misguide us. Or as Nicholas Baume notes in his essay: "The difference between a

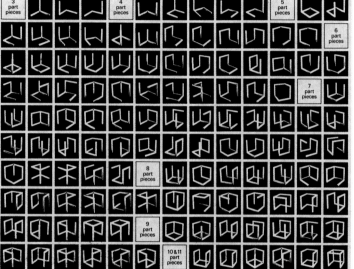

CAT.67

8-12

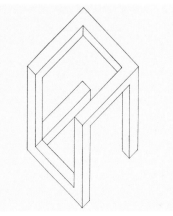

8-13

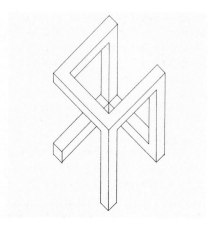

CAT.66

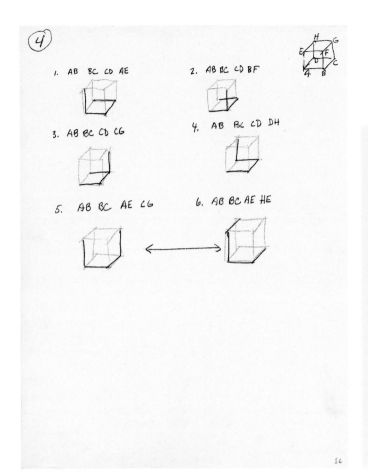

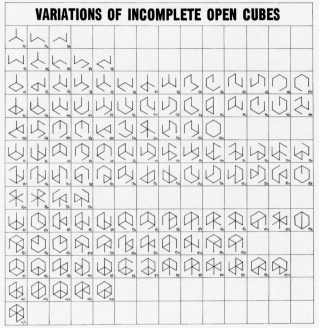

mirror image, which is not identical, and a repetition rotated so that it appears to be different, is often difficult to discern." In short, the complete cube is so easy to perceive and recognize immediately that one is surprised not only by the number of incomplete open cubes, but by the difficulty of perceiving and distinguishing among them. The viewer intuits an order but, as Bochner wrote, it is quite difficult to apprehend: "one is overwhelmed with a mass of data."

The layout of the cubes in the schematic drawings and in the smaller three-dimensional version seem to increase the difficulty of perception. Although LeWitt may insist that *any* layout is strictly speaking correct (so long as the cubes with same number of elements are kept together) it is nonetheless instructive to notice the difference between the working drawings and the final schematic drawings. When one examines the working drawings, one can see that LeWitt usually works with a system that makes it as easy as possible to discern differences between each cube and to see where duplicates are generated. For example, in a working drawing where LeWitt is working out the four part variations (cat. 12), the three part base is oriented in the same direction from cube to cube, making it quite simple to see how the variation works. One can see easily and precisely how each cube is different from the previous one. However, in the schematic drawing (cat. 65), the cubes are oriented in a way that makes it more difficult to see the variation from cube to cube; the bases are rotated in different directions, mirrored pairs are sometimes established, sometimes not. In the selection of systems themselves and in the presentation of the art LeWitt seems to have a definite preference towards emphasizing the tension between perception and conception. It should be noted that this gap is at work not only in the smallest version (2 5/8 x 2 5/8 x 2 5/8"), where all 122 incomplete cubes are exhibited as a single piece, but also in the book, the schematic drawings, and the largest versions (40 x 40 x 40"). With the larger cubes, the space between generality and particularity is held open inasmuch as you know there is a totality, but the size — and the worldwide distribution — of the object prevents one from perceiving it through the object itself; one has to make a leap to the concept.

While LeWitt's art emphasizes the gap between the perception of the object and the comprehension of the concept that produced it, the viewer can always bridge the gap. In this sense, the LeWittian aesthetic experience echoes the Kantian sublime, where an initial moment of being overwhelmed is followed by a moment of containment and representation of that which was formerly overwhelming because of its sheer size or its unimaginable force.[47] The experience of LeWitt's work — in a work like the cube series or in a wall drawing such as *Lines Not Straight Not Touching* — is distinguished from the Kantian sublime however by the fact that it is not the infinite and unrepresentable which overwhelms one at first (as in the sublime) but rather a large finite number. Here, we do not have the romantic experience of triumph as the power of our mind defeats the terror of being overwhelmed. Rather, we are momentarily stupefied by a mass of perceptual data that remains in tension with a relatively simple conceptual schema that organizes that data. The experience is more like what Sianne Ngai has called the "*stuplime*:" "in experiencing the sublime one confronts the infinite and elemental; in stuplimity, one confronts the machine or system, the taxonomy or vast combinatory, of which one is a part."[48] The sublime pretends to be universal and transcendental, the stuplime is more modest, but also more directly relevant to the social experience of modernity and modernization.

The relation that LeWitt establishes with the processes of modernization is that of a homeopathic negation. In order to neutralize them, LeWitt incorporates elements of the industrial process into both the production of the artwork and into the aesthetic experience of the work. Like Warhol, LeWitt references and mimics the industrial work process. In LeWitt's famous formulation: "When an artist uses a conceptual form of art, it means that all of the planning and decisions are made beforehand and the execution is a perfunctory affair. The idea becomes a machine that makes the art." The idea is a "machine" in the sense that it works automatically without any subjective input. "To work with a plan that is preset is one way of avoiding subjectivity."[49] The planning and execution are as rigorously divided as in a factory where the workers have neither time nor liberty to plan or think creatively about their task. The labor of producing the object itself involves technical skill, but no creativity, taste, or subjective decisions. This of course is the structure of rationalized labor, which is alienating precisely to the extent that the worker's subjectivity is unrecognized in the work process and indeed is destroyed as it forces the worker to become, as Marx argued, an "appendage of the machine."

LeWitt's conceptual approach is designed to duplicate a similar division of labor between planning and execution. In the production of the serial structures and the wall drawings alike, LeWitt willingly embraces the moment of being worked mechanistically, following an automatic course according to a preset logic. But, in mimicking the industrial production process, LeWitt recreates it "distorted in the state of resemblance."[50] Where the rationalized work process is designed to maximize efficiency and predictability, LeWitt champions the "irrational thought," for it is the "irrational thought" when followed "absolutely and logically" that can produce "new experience."[51] Irrational ideas are precisely those that are unpredictable,

47.
Kant's examples were mostly from nature – mountains, the Milky Way, a huge sea storm. The classic art historical representation of the sublime would be those Turner paintings of a very small boat in a huge sea, or the paintings of the Hudson River School of small people in the midst of an immense valley or mountain setting. Here is Kant's description of the phenomenon: "[What happens is that] our imagination strives to progress towards infinity, while our reason demands absolute totality as a real idea, and so [the imagination,] our power of estimating the magnitude of things in the world of sense, is inadequate to that idea. Yet this inadequacy itself is the arousal in us of the feeling that we have within us a supersensible power; and what is absolutely large is not an object of sense, but is the use that judgment makes use naturally of certain objects so as to [arouse] this (feeling), and in contrast with that any other use is small. Hence what is to be called sublime is not the object, but the attunement that the intellect [gets] through a certain presentation that occupies reflective judgment. . . *Sublime is what even to be able to think proves that the mind has a power surpassing any standard of sense. Critique of Judgement* trans. Werner Pluhar (Indianapolis: Hackett Publishing Company, 1987), p. 106.
48.
Sianne Ngai, "Stuplimity: Boredom and Shock in 20th Century Aesthetics," *Postmodern Culture*, published by Johns Hopkins University Press online, vol. 10, no. 2 (January 2000): p. 14.
49.
LeWitt, "Paragraphs," p. 79.
50.
Walter Benjamin, "The Image of Proust" *Illuminations* (New York: Schocken Books, 1968), p. 205.
51.
LeWitt, "Sentences on Conceptual Art," *LeWitt: Critical Texts*, p. 88.

wasteful and "purposeless." In LeWitt's work the division of labor is a technique for producing surprise, in a manner, moreover, that is highly inefficient. LeWitt remarks that "The artist cannot imagine his art, and cannot perceive it until it is complete."[52] The point of the compositional division of labor is to enable a moment of surprise, the surprise of perception unanticipated by and in tension with the conception. And as one can see in the working drawings for the "incomplete open cube," when one decides in advance to follow an idea "absolutely and logically" it can produce unexpected amounts of labor. Hence, LeWitt can say that he is "always surprised and never really surprised:"[53] always surprised in the sense that one never can predict the nature of the perceptual experience from the concept, and never surprised in the sense that this gap or rupture between concept and perception can be adopted as a general rule.

In essence, LeWitt dissevers the process of rationalization from rationality. He re-directs the basic principles of the Fordist factory — systematic simplification (the reduction of "infinite to finite information loads") and the treatment of the human body as a systemic machine. Like Warhol, LeWitt reappropriates a mode of operation from the world of industrial capital and distorts it, defamiliarizes it and puts it to a different use. His work is a kind of lesson in the way that systematicity and mechanicity — which at times seems wholly in service to means-ends rationality and the efficient production of predictable and hence profitable commodities — can be used to produce surprises. These surprises, I will now argue, are pleasurable precisely to the extent that they homeopathically neutralize elements of an everyday life defined by "functional differentiation."

THE NEGOTIATION BETWEEN perception on a local level and the total system that organizes that perception is not unlike the individual's experience of urban space. This is especially true in an urban space like Manhattan, where the grid system — in its conceptual totality — that we keep in our head allows us to negotiate city space even when we do not know where we are by experiential knowledge or visual recognition. In a place like Manhattan, the finiteness of the grid, constituted by the edge of the island, helps in this locating; it is not infinite space in which we are locating ourselves. As in LeWitt's systems, there is predictable, systemic variation, within a large finite totality. As a shorthand for this ability to have an image in our minds of the city which we are negotiating, an image that gives us a sense of direction and location, Fredric Jameson, borrowing from Kevin Lynch's influential *Image of the City*, uses the term "cognitive mapping." We might distinguish, however, as Lynch does,[54] between a city in which one locates oneself according to the anonymous grid and one in which monuments, nodes, boundaries, and landmarks do the work of helping in "the construction or reconstruction of an articulated ensemble which can be retained in memory and which the individual subject can map and remap along the moments of mobile, alternative trajectories."[55] The difference is that the grid requires little or no perceptual, experiential knowledge of the place: with the grid there is a gap between the total structure organizing the space and the perceptual experience of it. In a non-grid city like Boston, with helpful points of reference like the Charles River, Boston Common and Boston Harbor, one acquires a cognitive map of the city through repetitive experience of it. The grid, we might say, is a system developed

52.
LeWitt, "Sentences," p. 89.
53.
Sol LeWitt, public discussion with Gary Garrels and Andrea Miller-Keller, San Francisco Museum of Modern Art, 19 February 2000.
54.
Kevin Lynch, *The Image of the City* (Cambridge: MIT Press, 1960).
55.
Lynch's examples are Boston (non-grid) and Jersey City (grid).

for organizing large, finite bodies of information, and in New York, a way to reduce information loads in a city space where information loads are maximal. Lynch emphasizes the emotional effects of our ability to produce a cognitive map. Since an image of the total system in which one is located is of course a crucial element in establishing one's confidence in one's ability to live in the world — see friends, go to concerts, go out to dinner, get to the train station — the lack of such an ability can produce a sense of anxiety, loneliness, and alienation. LeWitt's *Incomplete Open Cube* series at once references this moment of alienation and resolves it; it reproduces the difficulty of acquiring a cognitive map as well as the pleasures of having one.

We begin to see the social significance of LeWitt's conceptual approach when we remember that it is not only our cities of which cognitive maps are helpful. We need and desire cognitive maps of social space as well, of the social structures, systems and institutions that we must also negotiate on a daily basis. Such a map's function is "to enable a situational representation on the part of the individual subject to that vaster and properly unrepresentable totality which is the ensemble of society's structures as a whole."[56] In other words, we are speaking of particular mode of ideology, one way of representing our "imaginary relationship to real conditions of existence" (in Althusser's classic formulation).[57] Just as one needs a cognitive map of city space in order to have a sense of agency there, one requires a cognitive map of social space for a sense of agency in the world more generally. Its lack can produce a sense of anxiety, isolation, and immobility. As life is less and less determined by local contexts and the gap between system and experience grows ever greater such a feeling has become more and more difficult to secure. Modernization could be seen as a process which continually widens the gap between individual experience and the systems which structure and enable that experience. If colonialism meant that the truth of life in the metropolis was in some way determined in and by the colonies themselves (that is, quite far from a local context), then today globalization has made the gap even more substantial.[58] Today, the systems which constitute our lives and on which we rely in innumerable ways are even more diffuse, multiple, and distant. No one of us has the comprehension of the overall system that structures our daily life world. The complexity not only of the operation of the very computer on which I am writing this essay but also of the global economies which enabled its production and affordability for me — these complexities I could maybe comprehend if I now devoted my life to the task. But this would not change the fact that my daily life is constituted by an aggregate of orders and systems neither I nor anyone else can comprehend.

In such a context, the function of ideology is to pretend that in fact the universal context in which daily life is to be understood *is* readily accessible, there at hand, or that there is not really much *to* understand. Often, as we all know, it is consumption itself that promises to assuage one's anxieties and place one's life in an immediately understandable and meaningful context. And such pleasures are hard to resist. But the fact that my computer was assembled in Taiwan, the wage that workers were paid to assemble it, the fact that these wages are kept low by practices actively supported by my government, for example, these things are nowhere to be found in the consump-

56.
Jameson, *Posmodernism*, p. 51.
57.
Louis Althusser, "Ideology and Ideological State Apparatuses," *Lenin and Philosophy* (New York: Monthly Review Press, 1971)
58.
On this, Jameson writes, "Colonialism would constitute a pivotal moment in that history, the moment when "the truth of [daily] experience no longer coincides with the place in which it takes place. The truth of that limited experience of London lies, rather, in India or Hong Kong; it is bound up with the whole colonial system of the British Empire that determines the very quality of the individual's subjective life. Yet the structural coordinates are no longer accessible to immediate lived experience and are often not even conceptualizable for most people." Jameson, *Postmodernism*, p. 411.

tion context. There is no profit to be found in encouraging me to think about these problems. On the contrary, these are the facts that lead to protest. These are the sorts of things that the people protesting the World Bank and the IMF in Seattle and Prague are thinking about.

> THE MAN WITH LEISURE HAS TO ACCEPT WHAT THE CULTURE INDUSTRY OFFERS HIM. KANT'S NOMINALISM STILL EXPECTED A CONTRIBUTION FROM THE INDIVIDUAL, WHO WAS THOUGHT TO RELATE THE VARIED EXPERIENCES OF THE SENSES TO FUNDAMENTAL CONCEPTS; BUT INDUSTRY ROBS THE INDIVIDUAL OF HIS FUNCTION. ITS PRIME SERVICE TO THE CUSTOMER IS TO DO HIS SCHEMATIZING FOR HIM. KANT SAID THAT THERE WAS A SECRET MECHANISM IN THE SOUL WHICH PREPARED DIRECT INTUITION IN SUCH A WAY THAT IT COULD BE FITTED INTO THE SYSTEM OF PURE REASON. BUT TODAY THAT SECRET HAS BEEN DECIPHERED. . . . . THERE IS NOTHING LEFT FOR THE CONSUMER TO CLASSIFY. PRODUCERS HAVE DONE IT FOR HIM.[59]

In their influential essay on mass culture, Adorno and Horkheimer argue that the function of mass culture is to do the work of making the world seem instantly comprehensible in terms already available in order to make consumption easy and self-affirming and to prevent critical thought.

Even if I do not agree with their sense of the total domination of mass culture to the exclusion of any possible resistance on the part of the consumer, I reference Adorno and Horkheimer here because they offer what I take to be a more or less received notion regarding mass culture's dominant paradigm. They are speaking of the way that Hollywood films and popular music are standardized into completely predictable forms. The ending of the movie, the length and pace of the sitcom, the placement of the chorus in a song all follow forms that we know instantly because they correspond to preset formulas. There is nothing left for the consumer to classify. Extensive market research and focus groups mean that mass culture offers us what we want before we have even thought about it. In this formulation, the mass cultural text produces no tension with any universal since it inevitably matches up with it exactly. In order to be attractive, easy-to-view and recognizable, mass culture must work, as Adorno and Horkheimer put it elsewhere, in the "worn grooves of association." Above all the consumer must never be surprised or confused.

59.
Horkheimer and Adorno, "Mass Culture," pp. 124-5.
60.
Fredric Jameson, *Late Modernism: Adorno, Or the Persistence of the Dialectic* (New York: Verso, 1990), p. 168.

In this world LeWitt's work constitutes a stoppage, an interruption. This is the reason that the surprise his work produces is pleasurable. In our everyday lives, we all experience the difficulty of matching up our daily experience with an understanding of the structures that make that experience possible. Adorno and Horkheimer, I think rightly, argue that one of the primary functions of mass culture is to disavow this difficulty. In contrast to this everyday world, LeWitt offers us the chance to experience this contradiction between the general and the particular; and what a relief it is to find a place to experience that set of emotions. But, LeWitt also offers us a feeling for what it might be like if the overall principle organizing perceptual experience *could* be understood, if we the viewer had the power — as we always do in a LeWitt work — to think about the perceptual and the conceptual in relation to each other, even if that relationship is contradictory or paradoxical.

Here we can see the social significance of what Rosalind Krauss called LeWitt's "absurd nominalism." LeWitt's work is nominalist insofar as it resists the forms of universality already present in the world — namely the universality of universal equivalence. But he does not reject the universal outright; rather he homeopathically incorporates "the universal" as a kind of empty signifier into his art in the form of the idea that is the machine that creates the art. Adorno argues that a nominalist art is the only art that can resist the forces of the commodity and mass culture that he wrote about with Horkheimer.

> NOMINALISM HERE DISSOCIATES THE REMNANT OF LIVED IMMEDIACY ITSELF FROM ITS 'UNIVERSAL', WHICH HAS NOW BECOME THE UNIVERSAL EQUIVALENCE AND ABSTRACTION OF THE COMMODITY FORM: THE WORK OF ART, HOWEVER, STUBBORNLY HOLDS ON TO BOTH, IN ORDER TO PRESERVE THE TRUTH OF THEIR CONTRADICTION. . . . . THE COMMODITY FORM, THEN, IS TO THE SITUATION OF NOMINALISM AS THE FALSE UNIVERSAL TO THE BEREFT PARTICULAR: THE FORMER'S EMPTY ABSTRACTION DETERMINES A HETEROGENEITY OF ISOLATED DATA — WHETHER IN THE WORLD OR THE SELF — THAT CAN NO LONGER BE MADE TO *MEAN*, IF ONE UNDERSTANDS 'MEANING' IN THE TRADITIONAL WAY AS THE SUBSUMPTION OF A PARTICULAR UNDER A GENERAL.[60]

To bring this notion of nominalism to the *Incomplete Open Cube* series, we might say that in that work, the "lived immediacy" of the cubes is dissociated from the total concept of the series as a whole, but the concept is still there across a gap, preserving "the truth of their contradiction." LeWitt's work reproduces the desire for and experience of a universal, but in such a way that marks the discontinuity between LeWitt's system and the systems at work in the everyday lifeworld. In this sense LeWitt's is an avowedly false universality, quite different from the ideological false universality of mass culture, which pretends to be real. In this sense, it is mass culture that produces the optical illusion and LeWitt who unravels it. LeWitt's systems are like props designed to generate the *feeling* of pleasure one gets from a group of objects organized by a total system. While refusing to give in to the universal of universal equivalence embodied in the commodity form, LeWitt's work nonetheless holds out the possibility of a total system. Here again, LeWitt's systems resemble but distort the commodity system. Instead of producing equivalences, LeWitt's systems produce *variation*. And LeWitt's variations resist exchange, they resist an abstraction that would make them equivalent with each other.

To move towards conclusion, we might say that where Warhol's art is about likeness and liking — group affinities formed though likeness — LeWitt's is about group affinities formed through variation in relation to a system. This principle can be seen best in the *Incomplete Open Cube* series. There, all 122 incomplete cubes are different from each other in a predetermined way. They are each unique. In a way quite different from Warhol, this makes LeWitt's seriality also about "likeness." Here, however, likeness is achieved through a shared lack. What the cubes all share is their incompletion, their lack of cube-ness. One might say that the cubes form a melancholy community — they are all missing the same thing, but each in a different specific way. And like Freud's melancholic, each incomplete cube has introjected its loss; each cannot help but signify its lost cube. However — and here is one of the sources of the pleasure of the piece — the cubes are not alone in their loss; in fact, it is *loss* that brings them together. Being brought together by what they are missing, they form a kind of diasporic community. This structure of affiliation has the advantage of preserving particularity. It is also a form of affiliation that can easily support collective opposition, and as such it may be especially apt for the present historical moment. It is, for example, what brought the various activists together in the protests against the World Trade Organization in Seattle. Trade unions, environmentalists, anarchists, socialists, post-colonials were brought together to protest global capital not because they shared anything essential — the diversity of the protesters was widely noted — but because they all felt equally subject to the systematicity of global capital. In an abstracted way, LeWitt's work reproduces the feeling of this sort of a melancholic community — the feeling of affiliation created through a shared negation. Thus the attraction, the emotional-historical force motivating us to give in to the idea-machine that produces the work, can be stated in the following way. By letting the idea be the "machine that makes the art" LeWitt is able to produce art that helps us to remember not only what it feels like to be aware of the machines that order our everyday lives. *Variations of Incomplete Open Cubes* also reminds us that the alienation that is an inevitable effect of being part of the machine-assemblage can also be transformed into the basis of affiliation, even collective opposition.

Adorno once remarked that "the feelings provoked by artworks are real and to this extent extra-aesthetic."[61] He was speaking of the fact that it is through their emotional effects that artworks exceed themselves, contradicting their own apparent disinterestedness and autonomy. One might make the case that inasmuch as emotions need contexts and objects in order to come into existence, artworks allow emotions to come into existence in forms that otherwise might not exist. This is the locus of their political importance. While LeWitt and Warhol have quite different strategies for bringing unexpected emotions into existence, being machine-like for both of them is about reorienting us in relation to our affects, providing us with alternative maps of our affective worlds. The paradox at the center of both of their projects is that the negation of subjectivity achieved through the imitation of the machine does not increase our alienation; instead it rescues us from our isolation by reminding us to notice our likenesses.

The author would like to thank Danielle Aubert, Philip Harper, Tan Lin, Eric Lott and Howard Singerman for helpful feedback and suggestions on earlier drafts of this essay. Thanks also to Marcia Hinckley for her invaluable editorial advice. One of the great pleasures of writing this essay has been the conversations it has allowed me to have with Carol and Sol LeWitt. Many thanks to the LeWitts, and to Sol LeWitt in particular for several illuminating conversations about his work. Finally, much gratitude is owed Nicholas Baume for inviting me to write this essay, for frequent late night counsel and insightful editorial assistance.

61.
Adorno, *Aesthetic Theory*, p. 269.

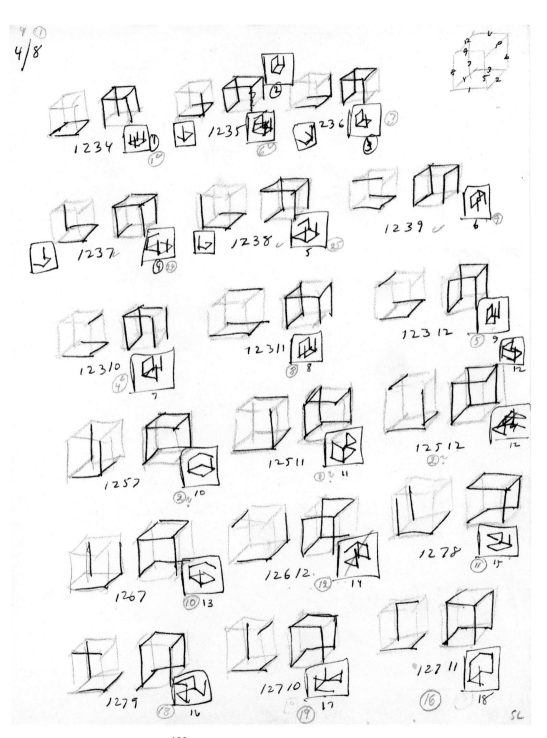

4/8

1234 1235 1236
1237 1238 1239
12310 12311 12312
1257 12511 12512
1267 12612 1278
1279 12710 12711

CAT. 19
WORKING DRAWING FOR FOUR- AND EIGHT-
PART INCOMPLETE OPEN CUBES (NUMERICAL),
1973-74
INK AND PENCIL ON PAPER
1 OF 2 PARTS, 11 X 8 1/2" EACH
THE LEWITT COLLECTION,
CHESTER, CONNECTICUT

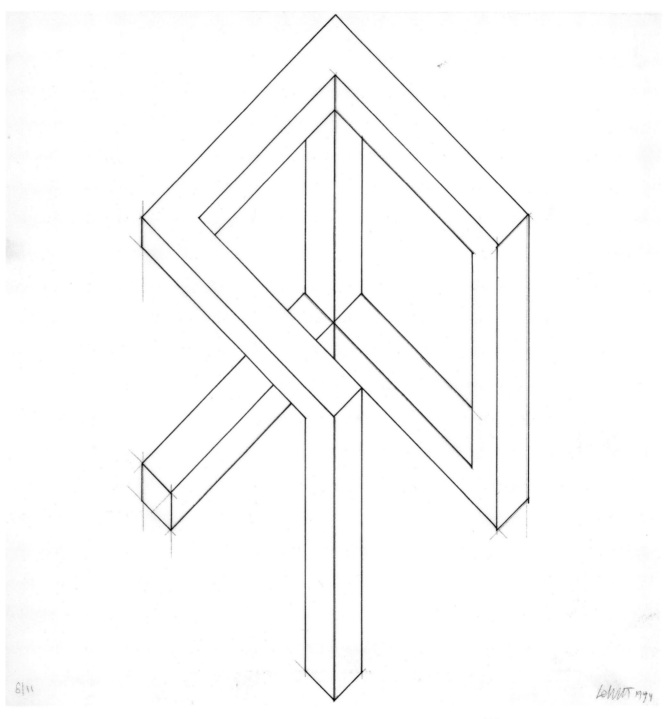

CAT. 33
8/11 FROM
SCHEMATIC DRAWINGS FOR
INCOMPLETE OPEN CUBES, 1974
INK AND PENCIL ON VELLUM
131 PARTS
12 X 12" EACH
THE LEWITT COLLECTION,
CHESTER, CONNECTICUT

8/11

LeWitt 1974

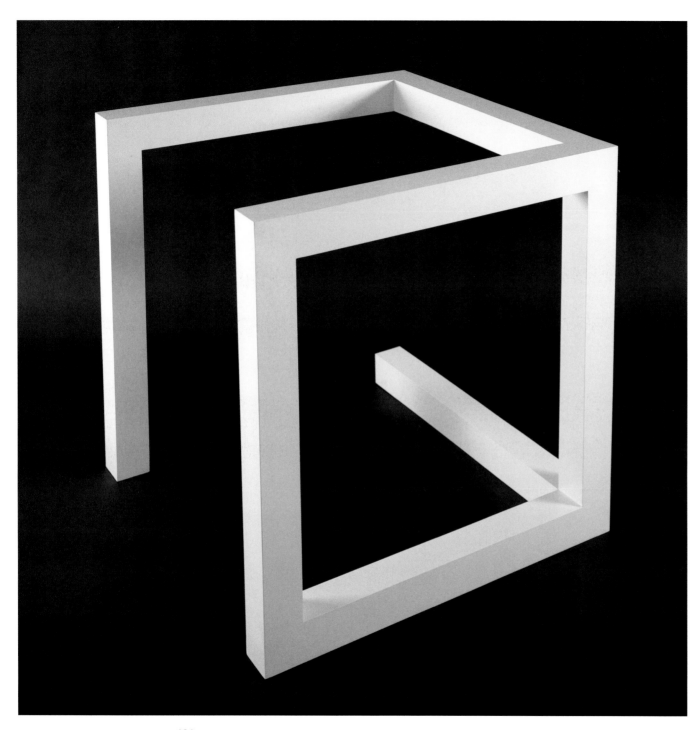

CAT. 59 - VIEW 1
INCOMPLETE OPEN CUBE 8/11, 1974
PAINTED ALUMINUM
42 X 42 X 42"
PRIVATE COLLECTION, SAN FRANCISCO

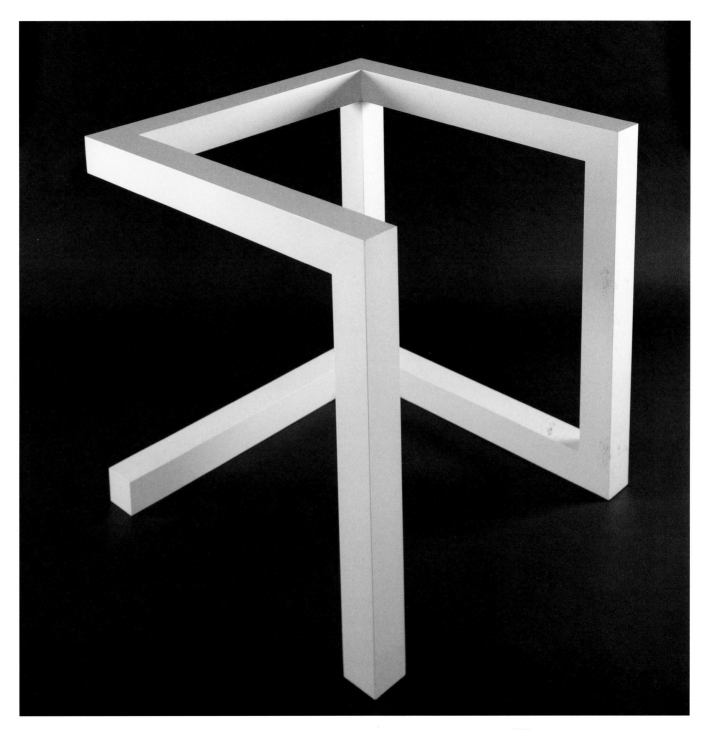

CAT. 59 - VIEW 2
INCOMPLETE OPEN CUBE 8/11, 1974
PAINTED ALUMINUM
42 X 42 X 42"
PRIVATE COLLECTION, SAN FRANCISCO

9/11

S-Lewitt

CAT. 33
9/11 FROM
*SCHEMATIC DRAWINGS FOR
INCOMPLETE OPEN CUBES*, 1974
INK AND PENCIL ON VELLUM
131 PARTS
12 X 12" EACH
THE LEWITT COLLECTION,
CHESTER, CONNECTICUT

106

CAT. 63
INCOMPLETE OPEN CUBE 9/11, 1974
PAINTED ALUMINUM
40 X 40 X 40"
DOUGLAS S. CRAMER

CAT. 33
11/1 FROM
SCHEMATIC DRAWINGS FOR
INCOMPLETE OPEN CUBES, 1974
INK AND PENCIL ON VELLUM
131 PARTS
12 X 12″ EACH
THE LEWITT COLLECTION,
CHESTER, CONNECTICUT

1. *Modular Cube*, 1965
Painted wood
14 1/2 x 14 1/2 x 14 1/2"
The LeWitt Collection, courtesy of the
Wadsworth Atheneum Museum of Art,
Hartford

2. *Working Drawing for Incomplete
Open Cubes*, 1973-74
Ink and pencil on paper
7 3/8 x 5 1/2"
The LeWitt Collection,
Chester, Connecticut

3. *Working Drawing for Incomplete
Open Cubes*, 1973-74
Ink and pencil on paper
7 3/8 x 5 1/2"
The LeWitt Collection,
Chester, Connecticut

4. *Working Drawing for Incomplete
Open Cubes*, 1973-74
Ink and pencil on paper
7 3/8 x 5 1/2"
The LeWitt Collection,
Chester, Connecticut

5. *Working Drawing for Incomplete
Open Cubes*, 1973-74
Ink and pencil on paper
7 3/8 x 5 1/2"
The LeWitt Collection,
Chester, Connecticut

6. *Working Drawing for Incomplete
Open Cubes*, 1973-74
Ink on paper
11 x 8 1/2"
The LeWitt Collection,
Chester, Connecticut

7. *Working Drawing for Incomplete
Open Cubes*, 1973-74
Ink on paper
11 x 8 1/2"
The LeWitt Collection,
Chester, Connecticut

8. *Working Drawing for Seven-Part
Incomplete Open Cubes*, 1973-74
Ink on paper
11 x 8 1/2"
The LeWitt Collection,
Chester, Connecticut

9. *Working Drawing for Seven-Part
Incomplete Open Cubes*, 1973-74
Ink on paper
11 x 8 1/2"
The LeWitt Collection,
Chester, Connecticut

10. *Working Drawing for Seven-Part
Incomplete Open Cubes*, 1973-74
Ink on paper
11 x 8 1/2"
The LeWitt Collection,
Chester, Connecticut

11. *Working Drawing for Eight-Part
Incomplete Open Cubes*, 1973-74
Ink on paper
11 x 8 1/2"
The LeWitt Collection,
Chester, Connecticut

12. *Working Drawing for
Four-Part Incomplete Open Cubes
(Alphabetical)*, 1973-74
Ink and pencil on paper
11 x 8 1/2"
The LeWitt Collection,
Chester, Connecticut

13. *Working Drawing for
Five-Part Incomplete Open Cubes
(Alphabetical)*, 1973-74
Ink and pencil on paper
2 parts, each 11 x 8 1/2"
The LeWitt Collection,
Chester, Connecticut

14. *Working Drawing for
Seven-Part Incomplete Open Cubes
(Alphabetical)*, 1973-74
Ink and pencil on paper
3 parts, each 11 x 8 1/2"
The LeWitt Collection,
Chester, Connecticut

15. *Working Drawing for
Eight-Part Incomplete Open Cubes
(Alphabetical)*, 1973-74
Ink and pencil on paper
3 parts, each 11 x 8 1/2"
The LeWitt Collection,
Chester, Connecticut

16. *Working Drawing for
Nine-Part Incomplete Open Cubes
(Alphabetical)*, 1973-74
Ink and pencil on paper
2 parts, each 11 x 8 1/2"
The LeWitt Collection,
Chester, Connecticut

17. *Working Drawing for Seven-Part
Incomplete Open Cubes (Numerical)*,
1973-74
Ink and pencil on paper
11 x 8 1/2"
The LeWitt Collection,
Chester, Connecticut

18. *Working Drawing for Three- and
Nine-Part Incomplete Open Cubes
(Numerical)*, 1973-74
Ink and pencil on paper
11 x 8 1/2"
The LeWitt Collection,
Chester, Connecticut

19. *Working Drawing for Four- and
Eight-Part Incomplete Open Cubes
(Numerical)*, 1973-74
Ink and pencil on paper
2 parts, 11 x 8 1/2" each
The LeWitt Collection,
Chester, Connecticut

20. *Working Drawing for Five- and
Seven-Part Incomplete Open Cubes
(Numerical)*, 1973-74
Ink and pencil on paper
3 parts, 11 x 8 1/2" each
The LeWitt Collection,
Chester, Connecticut

21. *Working Drawing for Five- and
Seven-Part Incomplete Open Cubes
(Numerical)*, 1973-74
Ink and pencil on paper
11 x 8 1/2"
The LeWitt Collection,
Chester, Connecticut

22. *Working Drawing for Five- and
Seven-Part Incomplete Open Cubes
(Numerical)*, 1973-74
Ink and pencil on paper
6 parts, 11 x 8 1/2" each
The LeWitt Collection,
Chester, Connecticut

23. *Working Drawing for Ten-Part
Incomplete Open Cubes (Numerical)*,
1973-74
Ink and pencil on paper
11 x 8 1/2"
The LeWitt Collection,
Chester, Connecticut

24. *Working Drawing for Six-Part
Incomplete Open Cubes (Numerical)*,
1973-74
Ink and pencil on paper
11 x 8 1/2"
The LeWitt Collection,
Chester, Connecticut

25. *Working Drawing for Seven-Part
Incomplete Open Cubes (Numerical)*,
1973-74
Ink and pencil on paper
11 x 8 1/2"
The LeWitt Collection,
Chester, Connecticut

26. *Working Drawing for Six-Part
Incomplete Open Cubes (Numerical)*,
1973-74
Ink and pencil on paper
11 x 8 1/2"
The LeWitt Collection,
Chester, Connecticut

27. *Working Drawing for Incomplete
Open Cubes*, 1973-74
Ink on paper
11 x 8 1/2"
The LeWitt Collection,
Chester, Connecticut

28. *Working Drawing for Incomplete
Open Cubes*, 1973-74
Ink on paper
11 x 8 1/2"
The LeWitt Collection,
Chester, Connecticut

29. *Working Drawing for Incomplete
Open Cubes*, 1973-74
Blue, red and black ink on paper
11 x 8 1/2"
The LeWitt Collection,
Chester, Connecticut

30. *Working Drawing for Incomplete
Open Cubes*, 1973-74
Ink on paper (recto and verso)
11 x 8 1/2"
The LeWitt Collection,
Chester, Connecticut

31. *Incomplete Open Cube 3/1*, 1974
Black and white photograph,
ink and pencil on vellum
13 x 25"
The LeWitt Collection, courtesy of the
Wadsworth Atheneum Museum of Art,
Hartford

32. *Incomplete Open Cube 3/1*, 1974
Painted wood
8 x 8 x 8"
The LeWitt Collection,
Chester, Connecticut

33. *Schematic Drawings for Incomplete Open Cubes*, 1974
Ink and pencil on vellum
131 parts
12 x 12" each
The LeWitt Collection,
Chester, Connecticut

34. *Incomplete Open Cube 3/1*, 1974
Painted aluminum
40 x 40 x 40"
The LeWitt Collection,
Chester, Connecticut

35. *Incomplete Open Cube 3/2*, 1974
Painted aluminum
40 x 40 x 40"
Collection Paula Cooper

36. *Incomplete Open Cube 5/2*, 1974
Painted aluminum
40 x 40 x 40"
The LeWitt Collection,
Chester, Connecticut

37. *Incomplete Open Cube 5/7*, 1974
Painted aluminum
40 x 40 x 40"
Herbert Lust Gallery

38. *Incomplete Open Cube 5/9*, 1974
Painted aluminum
43 x 43 x 43"
Joan S. Sonnabend

39. *Incomplete Open Cube 5/12*, 1974
Painted aluminum
40 x 40 x 40"
Private Collection, New York

40. *Incomplete Open Cube 5/14*, 1974
Painted aluminum
41 x 41 x 41"
Sheldon Memorial Art Gallery
and Sculpture Garden,
University of Nebraska-Lincoln,
Olga N. Sheldon Acquisition Trust.
1985.U-3744

41. *Incomplete Open Cube 6/2*, 1974
Painted aluminum
40 x 40 x 40"
The LeWitt Collection,
Chester, Connecticut

42. *Incomplete Open Cube 6/4*, 1974
Painted aluminum
40 x 40 x 40"
Herbert Lust Gallery

43. *Incomplete Open Cube 6/9*, 1974
Painted aluminum
40 x 40 x 40"
The LeWitt Collection,
Chester, Connecticut

44. *Incomplete Open Cube 6/13*, 1974
Painted aluminum
40 x 40 x 40"
Karla and Walter M. Goldschmidt

45. *Incomplete Open Cube 6/18*, 1974
Painted aluminum
42 x 42 x 42"
The LeWitt Collection, courtesy of the
Wadsworth Atheneum Museum of Art,
Hartford

46. *Incomplete Open Cube 6/19*, 1974
Painted aluminum
40 x 40 x 40"
The LeWitt Collection,
Chester, Connecticut

47. *Incomplete Open Cube 6/23*, 1974
Painted aluminum
40 x 40 x 40"
The LeWitt Collection,
Chester, Connecticut

48. *Incomplete Open Cube 6/24*, 1974
Painted aluminum
40 x 40 x 40"
Herbert Lust Gallery

49. *Incomplete Open Cube 7/5*, 1974
Painted aluminum
40 x 40 x 40"
Private Collection

50. *Incomplete Open Cube 7/10*, 1974
Painted aluminum
40 x 40 x 40"
Private Collection

51. *Incomplete Open Cube 7/11*, 1974
40 x 40 x 40"
Painted aluminum
Weatherspoon Art Gallery,
The University of North Carolina
at Greensboro, Museum Purchase
in honor of Editha Carpenter

52. *Incomplete Open Cube 7/12*, 1974
Painted aluminum
40 x 40 x 40"
Collection Lockhart

53. *Incomplete Open Cube 7/17*, 1974
Painted aluminum
40 x 40 x 40"
The LeWitt Collection, courtesy of the
Wadsworth Atheneum Museum of Art,
Hartford

54. *Incomplete Open Cube 7/18*, 1974
Painted aluminum
42 x 42 x 42"
Bayly Museum, University of Virginia.
Museum Purchase with funds from the
National Endowment for the Arts and
the Membership Art Acquisition Fund.
1976.3

55. *Incomplete Open Cube 7/22*, 1974
Painted aluminum
42 x 42 x 42"
Private Collection

56. *Incomplete Open Cube 7/26*, 1974
Painted aluminum
40 x 40 x 40"
The LeWitt Collection, courtesy of the
Wadsworth Atheneum Museum of Art,
Hartford

57. *Incomplete Open Cube 8/1*, 1974
Painted aluminum
40 x 40 x 40"
Herbert Lust Gallery

58. *Incomplete Open Cube 8/3*, 1974
Painted aluminum
42 x 42 x 42"
Lent by The Minneapolis
Institute of Arts, Gift of
Mr. and Mrs. Miles O. Fiterman and
the National Endowment for the Arts

59. *Incomplete Open Cube 8/11*, 1974
Painted aluminum
42 x 42 x 42"
Private Collection, San Francisco

60. *Incomplete Open Cube 8/14*, 1974
Painted aluminum
42 x 42 x 42"
Hood Museum of Art, Dartmouth
College, Hanover, NH;
purchased through the Julia L.
Whittier Fund and a matching
grant from the National Endowment
for the Arts

61. *Incomplete Open Cube 8/20*, 1974
Painted aluminum
42 x 42 x 42"
Collection Wexner Center for the Arts,
The Ohio State University;
purchased with funds provided
by the NEA in 1976

62. *Incomplete Open Cube 8/25*, 1974
Painted aluminum
40 x 40 x 40"
The LeWitt Collection, courtesy of the
Wadsworth Atheneum Museum of Art,
Hartford

63. *Incomplete Open Cube 9/11*, 1974
Painted aluminum
40 x 40 x 40"
Douglas S. Cramer

64. *Incomplete Open Cubes*, 1974/1982
122 painted wooden structures and
pencil on painted wooden base
Cubes: 2 5/8 x 2 5/8 x 2 5/8" each
Base: 29 x 70 x 65"
The LeWitt Collection, courtesy of the
Wadsworth Atheneum Museum of Art,
Hartford

Publications:

65. *Schematic Drawing for Incomplete
Open Cubes*, 1974
Printed 4 page announcement for the
exhibition *Wall Drawings and
Structures: The Location of Six
Geometric Figures / Variations of
Incomplete Open Cubes*, John Weber
Gallery, New York, October -
November 1974
15 x 15" (unfolded)
The LeWitt Collection,
Chester, Connecticut

66. *Sol LeWitt: Incomplete Open
Cubes*, 1974
Artist's book, 122 pages
John Weber Gallery (New York) 1974
8 x 8 x 5/8"
The LeWitt Collection,
Chester, Connecticut

67. *Sol LeWitt: Incomplete Open
Cubes*, 1974
Printed 4 page catalogue
with 1 page insert
Art & Project (Amsterdam)
Bulletin 88, 1975
11 3/4 x 16 1/2" (open)
The LeWitt Collection,
Chester, Connecticut